The Crypt of Academe

by

John L. Brown

AN ENTRY FOR THE

Stephen Leacock Award

FOR HUMOUR FOR

<u>2009</u>

Trafford
PUBLISHING™

www.trafford.com
North America & international
toll-free: 1 888 232 4444 (USA & Canada)
phone: 250 383 6864 ♦ fax: 250 383 6804 ♦ email: info@trafford.com
The United Kingdom & Europe
phone: +44 (0)1865 722 113 ♦ local rate: 0845 230 9601
facsimile: +44 (0)1865 722 868 ♦ email: info.uk@trafford.com

10 9 8 7 6 5 4 3 2

universitas magistrorum et scholarium
(a community of teachers and scholars)

To the good health and memory
of all those who reside therein.

Acknowledgements

THE AUTHOR BENEFITED greatly from the help and support of Neil Agnew, Lucie Cantrell, Helen Ho and Jamie Crowe. Neil unwittingly planted the germ of an idea that resulted in this slim tome. He should not be blamed for the final product. Lucie's wit and support kept me at the task. Helen makes everything in my life worthwhile and a joy. Jaime's creativity and deft touch with the cartoons brought much of the shenanigans in the Crypt to life.

Contents

Introduction

HEREWITH ARE PRESENTED tales from the darkest depths of the Crypt of Academe as told by an old soldier no longer in the line of fire. Good thing too 'cause he'd no doubt fail that new political science course, Political Correctness 101. I understand it is now compulsory for all male faculty over 50.

I give you twenty episodes from life in the Crypt that concern the joys and woes of faculty and students, the major inhabitants of the Crypt. They include questions of evaluation of students and faculty, how faculty claw their way up the ranks, who wins the awards and why and how decisions get made, or more often don't.

So as not to bore the reader beyond sufferance I have tried to limit each episode to about five pages. Each one is presented in an unvarnished and straight forward manner without gilt or favour to anyone. No doubt I have left out topics and ignored arguments that some will think of as major and unforgivable omissions. Tough, it's my book so I get to pick. I have tried to be honest in my tales so if I offend tender sensibilities, again tough. You can't please everyone all the time and some at no time. But if I do bring a smile to the lips of a few and a pause for thought about the life and meaning of our Crypts, a.k.a. universities, even better.

I do have a few bona fides that legitimize my scribblings

on the dark secrets buried deep within the Crypt, protected from the external world by a deep and cold moat. It all started in my fearful days as a petrified undergraduate sitting in an introductory class taught by an ex-marine drill sergeant. OK, that is not exactly true but he looked and sounded like one and the effect was the same when he predicted the fate of a third of the class. He told us to look to the left and then the right because at least one of us would not be here next year. I had no doubt his gaze bore straight through me and my fate was sealed. Somehow I escaped and carried on through three more years to graduate with grades enough that helped me convince respectable graduate schools to let me darken their doors and eventually place the letters, Ph D after my name. And now to arrive at this juncture in my life penning my own modest thoughts on life within the Crypt.

When I first crossed the moat and marched through the portals as a fully anointed denizen of my first Crypt I had no idea what awaited me. I hope future innocents may benefit from my twenty-six years of experience in the ivory tower. In due time I experienced all of the available delights and rewards along with at least a fair share of the grief and travails that come with the territory.

I will admit at times I may have included a harsh word or phrase but when all is said and done I must and will confess that my life in the Crypt was a good one. I would go further and suggest that our Crypts are of unparalleled importance to the fabric of our life. At their best they contribute beyond measure to our intellectual, social, emotional, democratic and economic life. And any institution of such importance deserves periodic scrutiny from a variety of angles, including the tongue in cheek.

1

Episode

Creativity? Rarely

TWENTY-FIVE YEARS IN the trenches of academe and I didn't think any student scribbles would surprise me. Not even the time the 59 year old bald guy in my mature class started his essay on the 'Death of Inflation' with, "Shall I compare thee to a summer's day!" He knew it had nothing to do with the topic. It was his way of saying he liked me and hoped I would keep that in mind as I read his essay. I recalled Mark Twain's comment, "I can live for two months on a good compliment." Hell, I can live that long on a mediocre compliment. So I thanked him and read on.

It turned out the essay was more on death than inflation. I asked him why and he said there had been a lot of it in his family lately so he knew more about death than inflation. He thought it would be best if he stuck to something he knew. I gave him a 'C' for compassion. He kissed me on the cheek and when I looked in the mirror I noticed a preference for pink lipstick.

Nor did I succumb to surprise when Daphne the stripper joined my night class. She often showed up in her work gear under a white Burberry style trench coat, more copy than authentic I'm sure. She claimed she went straight to work after class and didn't have time to change. I didn't mind except on nights when some of the jocks in class turned up the heat so high we all wanted to strip down to our underwear. Daphne had no problem since she merely shrugged off her coat. The Dean stumbled in one day and raised hell until I convinced him it would be a violation of the Charter of Human Rights not to allow someone to show up for class in their work clothes. Showing his usual steely resolve in the face of conflict and confrontation he quietly retreated but not until his cell phone captured a memoir of Daphne's obvious assets.

I especially admired Daphne for plying her trade without the benefit of silicone enhancement. That takes no end of courage in her highly competitive and busty business. I'm sure her assets are real because I've had opportunity on many an evening after class for close personal observation watching her perform. Daphne always saved me a ring side seat.

Too bad she never finished my class. She didn't turn in her essay. I told her she had to give me something, anything, or it would be a grade of Incomplete. Maybe she will one day. I've left the file and the door open.

But my jaw dropped into my crouch when I picked up this year's first term essays. I noticed a few students missing from class that day but a quick count confirmed that the number of essays equaled the enrollment. I hate it when essays are missing or late. The problem is less the missing essay than the dreary and tearful excuses. Or the offer of other forms of compensation in return for a liberal view of the lateness or ignore it all together. Such offers include the odd, and I do mean odd, sexual favour from male and female students. In the interests of affirmative action I won't say which predominates, nor will I be so indiscreet as to reveal my response. But I have also had offers of a free week in a Maui condo and a bottle of world renowned Kentucky moonshine, better than any single malt, or so said the offeree. I still have a half bottle and find it makes a good enamel remover, of teeth or bathroom sinks.

My favorite bribe is a carved statue of the three brass monkeys, See no Evil, Hear no Evil, Speak no Evil. Except written underneath were the words, "Don't be a spectator. Do it."

I settled in that evening to get on with one of academic life's most unrewarding activities. Deciphering the scrawls and illiteracy of modern undergraduates. I once tried to shortcut the pain with what some call the gravity method of grading _ a quick flick of the wrist to send the essays hurtling down a flight of stairs. Watching the offensive bits of paper float through the air gave me an almost erotic feeling of elation and release. Post coital remorse soon set in when I had to gather them up. Some had come apart and the more numerically challenged students had neglected to insert page numbers. The jigsaw puzzle of reassembly produced more pain and anguish than if I had merely read them in an undisassmebled state. The fact that most students have no idea how to relate a set of ideas in any sort of logical order made the task even more of a challenge. Although I was never sure if they could have told the difference. To insure against possible challenges the grades surpassed my usually generous standard and I never heard from anyone.

It gave me further evidence that returned essays make a quick transition from grader, to student, to trash can.

I now use a reward schedule to get me through the agony. I have a variety of programs but my favorite is the Gaelic schedule _ after every ten essays I reward myself with a refill of a better than average single malt. Sometimes near the end of the ordeal I shorten the delay to every five essays so I can hang in until the bitter end. The cost goes but it promotes survival. Grading doesn't allow for both sanity and sobriety.

I had just finished the first ten essays and sweated the usual pint of hemoglobin and settled back with my glass fully refreshed. I picked up essay #11 and turned over the cover page. I read the first page three times. Not because it was written in a lost Middle Eastern language, nor did the syntax and presentation mangle Standard English. It was because what I read was the exact opposite of all of the above. I turned the page expecting reversion to form but met disappointment. I shook my head and refreshed my mind with a sharp intake from my glass of amber liquid. That did the trick. In a massive slap of déjà vu I knew where I had seen what I just read. It was an almost verbatim regurgitation of my lecture notes. I almost stroked in large red letters, PLAGIARISM but remembered Mark Twain and read on.

The essay transited from an ode to me to ideas even more brilliant and erudite. This time an almost verbatim borrowing from one of the award winning articles that is the basis of one of my lectures. By now I had relaxed and for the first time in recent memory enjoyed the reading of a student essay. As I moved on to the last few pages the writing remained of the highest quality as I might expect given the source but the pages turned glossy with colored diagrams. The author had given up on copying and merely appended pages from the original article. A good cut and paste job I must say but hardly according to the rules of independent scholarship. What to do? Procrastinate seemed the answer. And a refill of my glass.

I set essay 11 aside and turned over the first page of #12. It had a familiar ring but I couldn't quite identify the familiarity. Then it hit me like a dead fish in a dirty old sock. The essay started with the conclusion from #11 and followed the argument back to the beginning. The introduction of #11 became the conclusion to #12. It also followed the same format of a mix of paraphrasing me and well known articles and finally fitting in the original pages of the periodicals.

Funny how both papers followed certain logic and made sense in their own unique way. I might have given them decent marks except for the blatant plagiarism. Now what to do? Tilt my bottle of single malt seemed the obvious answer. The bottom was almost in sight and the few dregs left might even evaporate before my next grading session if I didn't do the necessary. I can hunt down the culprits in the morning after a certain long and deep sleep. And if I'm lucky delicious dreams of Daphne. Maybe the one with whipped cream, chocolate and a cherry on top.

2

Episode

The Tweedles

TOO BAD LAST night's scotch induced warm intestinal glow of comfort and security didn't carry over to the morning. At least restraint cut in in time to maintain abdominal tranquility. Well, the truth is more like I ran out. At least the effect is the same. In times of boozy induced grief I always find comfort in the wisdom of that icon of imbibers, W.C. Fields, who once said, or at least I'm led to believe once said: "I feel sorry for people who don't drink. When they wake up that is the best they'll feel all day." So I at least have one thing to look forward to today.

I surveyed today's class of the usual disinterested throng. Disheveled might work as a global description. If I could wave a wand and remove all the torn blue jeans and dirty tee shirts I'd have a room full of naked bodies clad only in baseball caps set at various angles. I don't know where the fashion started but I have yet to meet anyone who looks better in a baseball cap than without one. Now there is a worthy topic for an anthropological doctoral dissertation. I'd read it and probably more thoroughly than the examining committee.

More of the class showed up than usual, no doubt to retrieve their essays, or more to the point, their grades. I don't believe the topic of today's lecture had rolled them out of bed or wrenched them away from their computer games. I had thought of being kind and handing out the essays at the beginning of class but my perverse nature took over and I held back until the end. Anyone who wants their essay must listen to me for an hour. Or at least occupy space in the same room with me.

I did wind up the class a few minutes earlier than usual. I always contrive to end the class with a sharp noise. Kind of like a hypnotist startling subjects back into this world. I started one day when I noticed two students sleeping in their seats, eyes closed, mouth hanging open, sleeping the sleep of intellectually unconcerned after all their brethren had long since departed. At first I planned to wait and see how long it took for them to wake up but decided it would interfere with my morning activity _ coffee and a donut with Bambi, the department secretary. Actually her name is Betty. No, I don't call her Bambi to her face, or even Betty. She much prefers Star. It is all part of my strategy to see my work gets done first. So far it's working.

I returned the essays and made appointments with two of the disgruntled to discuss my grading. I knew the argument. "I worked so hard, I should have a better grade." Among my many failures in academe is getting across the simple idea that there is no necessary relation between sweat spilt and grade received. The quality of output receives the most weight. The meetings shouldn't take up a lot of time since the no show rate is in the neighbourhood of 50%.

I had gathered up my pile of yellow, almost parchment like lecture notes and fading overheads still almost visible, I must learn PowerPoint one day, when two students straggled in. One of each gender. I was already late for my rendezvous with Bambi so I tried to brush past them as if they had come early for the next class. Not to be. They closed ranks and blocked the door. I decided civility might gain more than neglect so I asked if I could be of assistance. The answer was affirmative if I had their essays. Since I only had two left I now knew the ownership of essays 11 and 12. Thinking I couldn't keep referring to them as numbers I asked their name. Tweedle they said. I looked at my class list and there they were _ Tweedle, D. and another Tweedle, D. You're right, their parents had the courage, or effrontery, take your pick, to call the female Dee and the male Don. Tweedledee came easy and Tweedledum only a short stretch.

Upon closer inspection I could see a physical likeness that spelled twins. It almost but didn't quite stretch to their clothes. Like their essays the dress of one could be described as the opposite of the other. Dee wore a green shirt with red polka dots and Dum (my term, not their's) a red shirt with green polka dots. Below she wore red pants with green stripes over red shoes and he sported green pants with red stripes almost hiding green shoes. Of course their headgear was the obligatory baseball cap. Dum liked a red one with a green visor facing forward and you guessed it, Dee a green one with red visor pointing aft.

Caught totally off guard and unprepared I did the only thing any rational person would do under the circumstances, I lied. I said their essays were in my office but had to rush off to a not-to-be-missed meeting. I would be free in an hour and could meet them in the sanctuary of my office instead of out here in an open field of combat without any natural cover. They agreed and I raced to meet Bambi, sweat running down my backbone. An anatomical appendage I think I lacked at the moment.

Bambi borders on that indeterminate middling age where a little medical and cosmetic enhancement and some dim lighting cause heads to turn. But I'm not sure if the same results would obtain in the bright sunlight of a summer morning before the sanding, filling and painting took place. Her latest discovery is botox. She is now so enamored that I'm not sure she doesn't have weekly applications. It gives her a permanent pucker that drives my fantasy world into a tailspin. That and her platinum hair and rounded 60s figure turned out into a form fitting red cashmere sweater would have made her major competition for Marilyn Monroe or Jayne Mansfield. Yep, I'm old enough to remember both in their heyday. Too bad Bambi was born 20 years too late.

It's also a shame that most people don't get past the epidermis Bambi. Me included I guess when you look at my nick name for her. Her down to earth common sense laps most of the puerile scientism of my self-professed learned colleagues. The only reason I tolerate my department chair is I know at evaluation and promotion time he invites Bambi for lunch to ask her opinion on the candidates. He knows she's the only person he can rely on as trustworthy without scores to settle and axes to grind.

So I told her my tale of the Tweedle twins. She wondered why I had a problem. The purpose of the essay was to see if the students understood a particular topic and could communicate it in a readable and creative why. Had they not done that? It was the first time I had walked away from coffee with Bambi with an unhappy stomach. And it had nothing to do with my scotch habit.

3

Episode

Creativity?
In the Eye of the Beholder

I FOUND CURT lolling outside my office door. What a prophetic choice of name. Everything about him drooped from his cap slouched over his forehead to his faded ripped jeans with the crotch somewhere in the neighbourhood of I guessed his knees. Since he had his cap on right way around I started out lending him the benefit of the doubt and placed him somewhere on the positive side of the IQ curve. I say lend because that way I can take it back without retribution.

I greeted him with I hoped a cheery, "Hey man, how ya' doin'." In return I got an almost audible, "K". In an attempt at levity I asked if he could answer a question about youth fashion. "O.K. if it's quick, I have to get to work," he replied. I recognized the priority and knew it did not include anything academic. In an effort to comply I blurted out, "Do you think the workers who put the rips in your jeans were male or female or do you think the companies are equal rights employers and use about half and half?"

"You serious," came back at me accompanied by a look of pity one might save for the idiots of this world, or should that be developmentally disadvantaged? "It's like your lectures, I don't understand a word." He then slumped in a chair without invitation and resumed a blank stare.

I pride myself on knowing when to change the topic to escape a difficult situation so I decided the time had come to get to the reason for the meeting and end it as soon as possible. I asked if he was here to discuss his essay grade and again he gave me a look of incredulity. Sort of like do you think I'd ever come by for a social chat? I had given him what I thought was a generous A minus so his presence surprised me and I said so. His explanation was his career path included law school and the minimum grade he could accept was a full A without any unnecessary qualifiers like a minus. I gave his essay another cursory flip through and was overwhelmed how it stretched the outer limits of pedestrian. I now understood his interest in law. I wanted to drop him somewhere into the B range but knew that was beyond my personal limits of bravery. I did summon up as much backbone as I could and affirmed that the grade would stand.

Stand is what Curt did and asked if that was my final word. I affirmed it was, with an addendum of 'Sorry'. He shook his head and mumbled over his shoulder on his way through the door, "I guess my turn comes at course evaluation time."

The introduction of course evaluations has added an entirely new dimension to the world of the professoriate. No more saying good-bye to the class at the end of term and heading off to the faculty club for a celebratory drink with colleagues. Now it is the fear and wonder of the results of the course evaluations. Recent technology elevates the panic to new heights. I'm sure some of my students have cell phones that work like web cams. My new horror is ridicule on a student blog or a website devoted to the embarrassment of those of us who can't put on Academy Award winning performances before the class.

I barely had time to regain a modicum of composure when a rhythmic rat-a-tat-tat announced the return of the Tweedle twins into my life. It was refreshing to have students knock and wait to be invited in rather than crashing my office door. I expressed sorrow that the university's largesse only allowed a single chair for visitors. That meant I conveniently ignored the other chair in the room piled high with books. It was not for me to confess it was my own defense against too much comfort for visitors who may tarry longer than my attention span could tolerate. The Tweedles kindly stated that it was a minor inconvenience and looked large enough for both of them. As a test they each perched on half and said it was comfy enough.

They both leaned forward expectantly and in respectful silence, I presume waiting for my pronouncement on their essay grade. Since I hadn't written anything on their papers, neither good nor the other way I tried to play for time and turn the tables by asking, "What grade to you think you should get?" They paused, looked at each other in I'm sure a telepathic exchange, I've heard that's possible between twins, and said in unison, "A". The answer did not surprise me nor did it help me decide what to do. So I stalled further.

I asked by what criteria they arrived at their answer. "Creativity, after all we are from the creative arts." I inquired how stapling together pages from published articles and heavy borrowing from my lectures constituted creativity. I had to agree when they asked if I did not think creativity was synonymous with originality, or simply newness. I also had to agree that I had never seen a paper presented as they had presented their's. But I returned to my primary line of defense of their heavy handed borrowing of the work of others. They asked was it not usual to quote the work of others and make reference to the ideas of others, with of course appropriate attribution. I immediately jumped in and said that is the exact point I had been trying to get across to them and how they should approach the essay. They immediately jumped on me, together, saying that is what they had done. To buttress their argument they interjected a quote from George Keller who had said, "Creativity, it has been said, consists largely of re-arranging what we know in order to find out what we do not know." They had just done it in an overt and imaginative way.

I had to admit that they had shown imagination and no lack of chutzpah as well. Tweedledum immediately joined the argument by noting that if I agreed they had shown imagination then I joined no lesser company than that of Einstein who had said, "Imagination is more important then knowledge." Now I had not only to refute the Tweedle twins but go up against one of the acknowledged geniuses of all times. I could see I was on a slippery slope and sliding closer to the bottom.

I finally said more out of exhaustion than conviction that I might see my way clear to give them an A minus on the grounds of chutzpah and sheer gall. They agreed that would work for them and then closed the deal when they told me that, Sir Arthur Conan Doyle had written on behalf of Sherlock Holmes that, "Mediocrity knows nothing higher than itself, but talent instantly recognizes genius." And they could see that I was clearly someone with talent. I could only harken back to Mark Twain and his wisdom on compliments.

The Tweedles departed, essays in hand with me soon after on my way to the Faculty Club for some bracing liquid reinforcement and solace with one of my drinking companions.

4

Episode

Everyone Needs A Friend

WE ALL NEED something to rely on. Something predictable that doesn't vary with the seasons, or prevailing winds, or whichever party is goosing our taxes. One of mine is Harvey. I know I can find him any day of the week after 2:00 p.m. in his corner of the faculty club staring out at the garden searching for what, one never knows. No doubt inspiration.

Harvey is like so many toiling the fields of academe. He came to us anointed with a pedigree from the 'right' graduate school, world ranked supervisor and a thesis pointing to a promising new line of enquiry. All of that got him tenure but the promising line of enquiry never fulfilled the promise. So Harvey remains an Associate Professors still holding out faint hope for a resurrection of the creative juices to produce the one last paradigm shattering article that will clear the hurdle to join our full professors' club.

Despite a broken academic heart he remains a genial

and jovial drinking companion on most days. I found him in his usual spot, a small jug of almost flat beer at the half way mark his momentary companion. Between sips of beer he chews and sucks on whatever writing implement is in his possession that day. It's his aural gratification now the anti-smoking storm troopers carried the day to remove any vestige of the olfactory offence, even in the remotest corner of the club.

Harvey was a dedicated smoker at one time _ pipe, cigarettes, cigar, anything that produced tar and nicotine. He led the charge to retain a corner refuge in the club for those who wish to freely exercise a right to inflict whatever damage they so desire on their body with a product sold freely and legally. Kind of like booze, soft drinks, fries and fried chicken. Unfortunately, he was cut down on the first ballot. I'm not exactly a dedicated smoker but did join the fray for reasons of principle. I agree that smoking is a health hazard but want to retain the right to decide myself if I wish to enjoy a cigar. I do not want self appointed do-gooders making that decision for me.

I dropped into the chair beside Harvey and he looked over waiting for me to say something. Such is the etiquette when one enters the inner sanctum of a respected other, the intruder speaks first. I offered my usual greeting, "Hey Harv, anything good happen today?" He gave me a sly smile and said, "Bambi said Hi to me today." Only Harv knows her nickname.

I carried my own small jug of beer. It is our well established practice to bring your own jug to the table. It saves the hassle of buying rounds or trying to settle the bill in anything close to an equitable fashion. I poured the beer into my glass with excess haste and about half frothed into a foamy head. "Like a little head with your beer," said Harv and laughed at his own lame joke. He always does that. To get even I told him about my encounter with the Tweedle twins. When he heard the names he claimed I was manufacturing the entire episode. I think I convinced him to the contrary but the skeptical look did not drop from his face. At least he harrumphed and slid deeper into his chair.

I told him how I resolved the issue and he called me a coward. He said I should have marched them right over to the office of the Dean of Students and had them expelled for cheating. I yelped and almost jumped out of my chair at what I considered a radical and insane proposal. I pointed out to him that is just the kind of reaction that would see me out on the street despite tenure. I'd be called up on the carpet for harassment, discrimination and general bad manners. No one wants to hear about that sort of thing. Think of all the time it takes to make the case, reply to and show up for appeals and then likely end up in court. No, the university would not thank me for such foolishness. It would do nothing for my reputation, bank balance or getting me closer to Daphne. If I wanted to get in trouble I would sooner it be for a Daphne liaison than pushing academic purity on the Tweedles.

Harvey said it was typical of the lack of backbone in today's Crypt of Academe. Everyone was too busy churning out conventional wisdom that fit the editorial policy of the so called respectable journals. All that counted was numbers. Publish, publish, publish and the more the better. And for the student side of the enterprise, spoon feed pabulum for the main course and high grades for dessert. That way you get off the chart student ratings. The ultimate result being promotion to full professor. And in the best of all possible circumstances a chaired professorship. Eureka, you've arrived.

I raised a finger in protest, only to be ignored by Harv, now in full verbal flight. He claimed to be one of the meager few upholding true academic values. He would not publish anything unless it made a significant and path breaking contribution. And in the classroom his role was to challenge the minds of the youth. Not pat them on the head and say how wonderful they are no matter what nonsense dribbles forth. So he remains in truth and honor an Associate Professor.

He finally stopped for a refreshing gulp that drained his beer glass. Before I got my mouth half open he was out of his chair and off to the bar for a refill. I was ready when he returned. Before he sat down I asked, "Who's been rubbing your butt with sandpaper?"

It seems the department chair had called Harv in for an unsocial chat. He had been reviewing Harv's recent teaching and publication record. He came up a few bricks short of a full load on both. The Chair told Harv point blank that with such low productivity the university wasn't getting a fair return from Harv's effort, or to be more accurate, lack thereof. However, since Harv had tenure he couldn't be fired, at least not without a lot of effort and opposition from the academic union. So the Chair adopted the time honored tradition and upped Harv's teaching load. The students will now get more Harv. I have never understood why universities decide that the way to punish underperforming professors includes punishing students.

Harv's main concern was not the extra work in the classroom. The increased teaching was only more introductory sections of a class he had already taught many times. It would just mean droning on before more students. No, what bothered dear old Harv was the ignominy of it all. Before long his colleagues would know he had been relegated to the deadwood brigade. As solace I bought him a double single malt and said I still respected him for his keen and incisive mind. He smiled and drained the glass.

5

Episode

A Feast of the Foolish

THEY STRAGGLED INTO the department meeting like the remnants of Napoleon's army trudging home through the winter snows of Russia after the debacle of Moscow. A somewhat dispirited and bemused group. Academics are proud of their self managed brand of governance. It is something they guard with a jealousy unknown even to Othello. What has always astounded and amused me is the minimal interest they show in participating. The first and often not always met challenge of a faculty meeting is a quorum to make it a duly constituted assembly.

It looked like we'd meet the challenge today. The requisite number of faculty shuffled in carrying bundles of papers to occupy themselves so attendance isn't a complete waste of time. For some it was papers or exams to grade, for others a paper that needed editing or one to be reviewed for some learned journal. After all participation is not of prime importance, just a warm bum in the chair and someone to

25

provide a poke in the ribs to raise your hand aloft at voting time.

No doubt attendance benefited from a major item on the agenda. The examination and review of how our department will respond to the central administration's new research ethics guidelines. It seems some careless moron has put us all in jeopardy by failing to inform a research subject about the downside of participating in his experiment. The mindless error was compounded when something of great importance intervened and he failed to hold a debriefing interview to search out any traumas. The student's mother apparently had the time to do so and also the time to show up in the president's office to snitch on the miscreant. I don't know why they can't just fire his ass out the door and leave the rest of us alone. But that is not to be. We will now have endless forms to fill out that surpass the limits of the most moribund bureaucracy typically found in academic institutions.

In an uncharacteristic display of unity the entire department found the guidelines offensive. Each member of the department nodded sagely to another and acknowledged that the room is full of ethical people, to a man, and that includes the minority female group as well. Such guidelines might be necessary where abuse does happen. The medical faculty comes to mind where they do drug trials on real people to who knows what effect, except the bottom line of the sponsoring pharmaceutical companies. And of course there is the Psychology department that coerces innocent and naïve undergraduates to participate in experiments that further belabour the obvious.

A variety of our assembled mass tottered erect to rail at the blasphemy being wrought upon our innocent and already overworked group. After all, who has the time to fill out the forms and search out the requisite authoritative signatures? Finding the time to write the grant proposal is tough enough when it is piled on crushing teaching loads and unproductive committee assignments. Who has the time to read, think, discuss and write papers that push back the frontiers of science to improve the pitiful lot of mankind? The true calling of any group of committed academics, like all those present in the room.

We all agreed something must be done but what, escaped a quick consensus. Various religions voiced their favoured option. A solitary meek voice offered the obsequious canine solution _ roll over on your back, legs in the air and capitulate. Sort of go along to get along so we can get on with the search for truth. It may come as no surprise that the speaker was shouted down and put in his place before his butt hit the chair. Yes, it was a male speaker.

The bikini solution came next. That is provide the minimum cover you can get away with and still meet the standard. The option received some shrift but in the end it became short shrift. It still seemed akin to agreeing and submitting to directives from the enemy central administration. Something that is anathema to any true academic, sort of like a reaction that is almost bred in the bone.

That of course led to the Rambo option. Someone, preferably an expendable administrator like a department chair or dean would be armed and sent into the fray to do battle with the administration dragons. The chosen champion would of course be armed with a full vote of confidence from the assembled mass. The most truculent of our group jumped to their feet in support, some with a clenched fist thrust into the air and murmurs of 'right on'.

Finally, Merlin, the wizard of our group, read old with long white hair and wire rimmed glasses sliding off his nose rose to his feet and waited for the din to die. That's why we call him Merlin, even though his real name is Herb. Of course to keep up with the times maybe we should switch to Dumbledore. In any event, back to Merlin/Dumbledore/Herb. Once he clearly held the floor and had all eyes in his direction he said we must return to our roots and remember true academic tradition when faced with such an attack. That is to fall back on the time tested alternative to ignore the whole damn thing until it goes away. Small coy smiles appeared and murmurs of assent buzzed through the room. What a brilliant solution and like all brilliant solutions, obvious once spoken. After all, what could be done since we nearly all held tenure.

That was until Beckett took the floor. We call him Beckett because as with Henry the Eighth he acts as our department conscience and yes butter. And like King Henry some of us wish him a similar fate to that of Beckett. This time he pointed out to us that to ignore the wishes of the central administration was not without cost. To obtain research grants we needed some of their signatures that would not likely be forthcoming if we choose to ignore them entirely. Without those signatures our applications would be dismissed without further thought. Now for those of us who had retired from the field of research it may be of no consequence but to others it would drain our life blood.

As expected, these were not words we wished to hear but they could not be ignored. A general debate followed, more accurately shouting match, as polite debate turned to jabs and sharp verbal elbows and old wounds were reopened in pursuit of past wars. Soon the topic became irrelevant and the battle was the thing. The exchange ground to a halt in the usual way. Not agreement but an examination of the clock indicated cocktail time had arrived, or for some with livers in danger, tea time.

There was still no resolution and the question of what was to be done remained. Of course we resorted to the time honoured solution of forming a committee and coerced some of our colleagues to serve. We pointed out to them that it wouldn't be an entire waste of time. It is always useful at annual review time because you can plead your lack of productivity comes from an overwhelming load of service to the department.

A few of our group smiled as we left the room. I asked if they liked the meeting and the outcome. One replied it was most productive, she had finished all of her grading. Another agreed that he had completely revised a paper and was ready to submit it for publication. They both then turned to me and asked if the meeting had come to any decision. I rose to my full height of six foot one, pushed my black beret onto my curly white locks and set it at a jaunty angle over my left eye and said, "The usual one." The reply came back, "Ah, who's on the committee this time."

6

Episode

Becoming Fireproof

TENURE, NO FUTURE without it. It is a rites de passage that fully anoints entry into the academic brotherhood. Or should that be personhood nowadays? I still remember mine so vividly it could have been yesterday, or more like this morning. Almost like my entire academic career from thesis defense, through tenure and finally promotion to full professor I suffered in doubt wondering if I was tall enough, smart enough and supported the winning political party.

I am wrenched back to reality when a look in the mirror reflects white hair, although with enough curl that some people think it comes from my Italian hairdresser. I affect a black beret as cover and to add what I think is a little continental je ne sais quoi.

I am now serving on the tenure committee of a young colleague and the entire tortuous ritual has changed little since my day. Of course a continuing vocal opposition to the very notion of tenure never goes away. The clamoring opponents, normally from beyond the moat of the Crypt of Academe see it as protection for the incompetent and early retired. The defenders, not surprisingly from inside the Crypt, see it as a bulwark that defends academic freedom and keeps the ill bred and uneducated beyond the moat and thereby ensures the pursuit of independent enquiry. More recent reliance on the purse of public companies to fund research weakens the force of this argument but not to the point of demise. Of course the argument is not helped by any and all universities establishing offices charged with hawking the application of recent research success.

From the outside the proceedings look exceedingly rigorous and certain to result in the 'correct' decision. Such revered institutions as impersonal and independent peer review without bias or forethought form the rock solid foundation. Right! Up close one observes the very personal decisions of a committee selected by such fallible human processes as contrived votes and selective appointments.

The starting gun fires with selection of the committee. Election puts internal department members like me on the committee but others are appointed by the dean and president's office to ensure we maintain the highest standards that give the university its presumed international renown. The preference of us internal folk is for the external reps to sit quietly, go along with the wisdom and knowledge appropriate to our department and demure to how we vote. Most of the time they do but not always. If they fall out of line the whole affair crumbles into a nightmare crap shoot.

As in most political systems our department is split into two main parties with the unimaginative titles of the 'Hards' and the 'Softs'. The Hards like whatever they can touch, count and weigh. The Softs think one should take a broader view and use personal wisdom and judgment to examine the whole person. The opposition is translated into the criteria to be considered for tenure.

For the Hards this means peer reviewed papers that appear in the top research journals read by a small and select group of the best minds in the field. More like stuck on a shelf by such minds. Teaching is recognized in the same way Churchill apparently treated vermouth in concocting a martini _ a nod to France.

The Softs want to be more eclectic and widen the net to include less easily measured criteria such as teaching, service to the profession and in the minds of the Hards even being kind to small animals and senior citizens.

As for myself I have been able to successfully adopt a Janus strategy and avoid most of the deadlier skirmishes. I do this by trying never to be in a room with a Hard and a Soft at the same time. And if I do and the going gets rough I make some comment about intestinal grief, fart and disappear into the nearest bathroom. A more accurate description of the intestinal grief would be, 'no guts'. In any event it removes me from harms way, even if I do have a questionable reputation as a social companion.

Once the committee is assembled a file is obtained from the candidate to include research contributions, teaching ratings and something called service which can be anything from committee assignments of any sort, public speeches and in one case I saw, shoveling snow for elderly neighbours. Well, why not, it is more clearly a service than membership on the organizing committee for some obscure conference attended by ten people, most of who went to graduate school together.

A cursory glance at the file left me confident all should

be over in a single and mercifully brief meeting. And most important I wouldn't have to read all the original material myself. I could rely on the summaries and reviews. The research reviews were in the order of solid scholar, bound to continue contributing and will make a valuable long term colleague. OK, not star quality but acceptable. The teaching ratings were enough above the norm to vote affirmative and more important no negative or threatening letters from students. I soon learned my glance had been too cursory and my confidence too hastily arrived at. One more review came in after I looked at the file.

The last review came from one of the leader's in the candidate's chosen field and also his Ph D alma mater. No doubt why he was chosen as a reviewer. The only other person of similar status was our candidate's thesis supervisor and obviously not eligible. The review contained words like trifle, of little interest, contains errors, best work is past him and likely came from his supervisor anyway and finally don't expect much from him in the future. Your best alternative is to offer him help in relocation to a lesser institution, or even better some obscure government bureau where he can do little harm.

I sat in my office pondering what to do and searching my memory to see if I could remove myself from the committee through a previously forgotten conflict of interest. A ringing phone interrupted my thoughts. It was the president's representative on the committee who wanted to discuss the latest news. He took it all very seriously and saw no way to support the candidate under the newly revealed circumstances. It seemed that what I thought was a situation where we could all go along and get along, followed by a celebratory drink at the faculty club was now out the window. Being completely bereft of ideas on how to escape I followed my usual avoidance strategy and went in search of Harvey at the faculty club.

A friend like Harvey is invaluable. He's easy to find and knows more of the institution's inner intrigue than I normally care about. But at times of crisis he often has the answer. I filled his glass from my own beer jug and told him the dilemma I faced. All I really wanted was a simple solution to get me off the committee. Instead I was read a tale that could have come from a cold war spy novel. It took Harv more than one attempt before I thought I understood the necessary details. He started to lose patience with my difficulties of comprehension and I had to buy him another jug to have him go over it one last time. It's hard to tell if the extra jug helped or hindered in the end.

But here is the gist of what he told me. Our candidate's supervisor and his reviewer may come from the same institution but have developed a feud to do justice to the Hatfields and McCoys. The problem worsened last year when the supervisor successfully intervened to deny tenure to the reviewer's protégé. He has been lying in wait for our candidate to come forth. A further twist is the president's rep on the committee and the reviewer were at grad school together and as undergrads were members of the same fraternity. There is no question how he will vote.

I sat down and scratched out the likely result. My department colleague on the committee will vote in favour because he and the candidate have a joint research proposal under consideration and he has a long history of recruiting junior faculty to service his research grants. He won't be left high and dry to do the work himself. The external member from the university is retired in all but name only and he will vote

35

yes to try and avoid attending appeals. The presidential appointee will vote negative and I can see his number on the call display of my ringing phone. In keeping with character I ignore the call.

If I too vote no the result will be a draw, throwing it all into the lap of the chair to decide. For our chair a fate worse than the bowels of Hades. But if I vote in favour the result will be 3-1 and the chair will readily reflect the will of the majority.

What to do? I am actually disposed to the young candidate but to stand up and vote in favour violates my Janus principles, if that word can be applied in this situation. I finally decide to do something I always avoid in these cases and retrieve the file from the chair's office. I may actually have to read all this stuff. Horror of horrors. But to my surprise I see an added entry that did not exist at last quick perusal. Acceptance of an article from the leading journal in the field with the most laudatory comments from the anonymous reviewers, although I'm pretty sure I can identify at least two of them.

I now have my out. I can and will vote in favour. After all to do otherwise would contradict the best of the best. I cannot do otherwise. A close escape for all of us. I have my out. The chair has his majority. The candidate is now tenured.

Upon reflection that was a close call. I must take more care in avoiding membership on such committees in the future. In fact all committees.

7

Episode

Climbing the Ladder

THE CAREER OF an academic follows a short hierar-
chy. There are only three steps. One starts at the bottom
rung as an assistant professor. If a candidate is successful in the following years, meaning publishes enough and
avoids outright riots in the classroom the expected outcome
is granting of tenure and swapping Assistant for Associate
Professor. The normal time to traverse this stage is around
six years, give or take a couple. The give or take depends
on pleading special circumstances usually related to health
or in recent years, maternity leave. On the rare occasion a
candidate may demand early consideration. The only ones
with the temerity to make such demands are distinguished
by youthful arrogance and an outstanding research record,
preferably accompanied by a lucrative offer from a more
prestigious institution. When one can at last reorder a new
set of business cards with the title Associate Professor it is a
signal of membership in the established order.

An assistant professor should be left alone to establish a research career and learn the subtle intricacies of classroom trench warfare. Only the foolish volunteer for, or allow themselves to be placed on committees of no purpose, which is all committees. They provide neither personal fulfillment, nor assets for advancement. As an Associate Professor that now changes. Unless you are hiding in a cave there are demands to see a service contribution on your annual report. Service to the faculty, service to the university, service to the profession and service to the community. It is expected and demanded. What's bizarre about it all is they rarely count for anything. But maybe that is the meaning of service. You shouldn't expect anything in return except a warm feeling in the nethers that one has been of service.

Despite the added service load the ambitious academic must still maintain a strong research record if she intends to breathe the rare ozone from the top rung of the ladder that is only occupied by those anointed and allowed to wipe the Associate from the business cards and leave the single word _ Professor.

Of course for folk whose bureaucratic experience is from beyond the moat and therefore not acquainted with the inner workings of the Crypt they often think there are further rungs up the ladder. Common mistakes are to grant unnecessary importance to the roles of Department Chair, Dean and President. Admittedly they do have certain powers and access to resources that may be used to gain their bidding. But for most of us their role is one of service. Look after the administrivia and see that we have adequate resources to fulfill our destiny i.e. get on with what we bloody well feel like in research and teaching.

I have twice gone over to the dark side and ventured into

the ranks of the administration. The first was reasonably pleasant as director of an international program. It relieved me of teaching and offered travel opportunities to exotic lands.

The second was as Associate Dean. The best candidates for such positions would come from the guard of a sultan's harem. It is best not to have balls for the job because if you do it doesn't matter since there is never an opportunity to put them to use. When a colleague in a similar position was asked what an Associate Dean did he chortled and replied, "Whatever the hell the dean doesn't want to do."

I lasted a few short months before the trivial stipend added to my salary and minimal reduction in teaching no longer provided adequate compensation. At the first opportunity I resigned in great righteousness on a point of principle and returned to the ranks of the professoriate.

We now had to assemble and decide if two of our colleagues had enough of the royal jelly to join our esteemed professorial rank. I have attended assemblies where the decision was simple and straight forward but only rarely. Usually there is some fly in the ointment to raise problems and ensure a protracted debate.

The process is similar to tenure. A file is assembled, a committee struck of internal and external reps and reviews are obtained from prestigious experts in the field. A decision is made followed by celebration or gnashing of teeth and moans of the inability of the established order to recognize true genius and innovation. The dean had caballed with the department chair to see that I was imposed upon the committee but I dodged my way out, claiming previous service on the tenure committee. The dean never misses a chance to shanghai me for a committee. I think it's because of long memory over my escaping as Associate Dean. I still couldn't get out of the meeting of full professors in the department to decide if the candidates are enough like us to be one of us.

One of the candidates is a friend of my buddy Harvey. They're friends because they share a similar fate, terminal Associate Professors. I've been dodging Harv of late because I know he wants to lobby for his chum. I'm sorry for that because I enjoy my beer time at the faculty club with Harv. I'm sure we can pick up shortly after the meeting. He'll grill me about what happened but I can duck behind confidentiality. He won't buy the argument but he'll go along to get along.

His friend hasn't let his name stand for promotion since I can't remember when. Rumour has it that the change of heart is acceptance of an article he has been flogging around the journals for eons. I'll learn soon enough.

By the time the meeting of full professors is held the likely outcome is known. The first was a clear acceptance. The only thing unknown is why the candidate hadn't been promoted earlier based on a record where outstanding leapt to the lips of most in attendance. In fact we may have waited too long. The word had passed through the ranks that she is being wooed by some of the best departments in the country. It did come up at the meeting. One of my less than drole colleagues suggested that maybe we could marry her off to someone locally who had no chance of getting a job elsewhere. I was the only single male in the room and my already fair complexion went many further shades of pale. I also felt insulted by the accusation of a lack of alternatives in the great outside world. A wiser member of the group pointed out that such a clearly sexist solution should not be passed on to the candidate or she would leave for sure, even if the idea had some practicality.

We then turned to Harv's buddy, not that I pointed that out, nor that I too am a friend of Harv's. The reviews turned out to be a mixed bag. Some slightly positive like, "early work showed promise, maybe it can be resuscitated." Some negative like "appears to have come to the end of his creative road, no doubt he can contribute in other ways, maybe as Associate Dean or some other minor administrative post." And a mix of waffle like, "recent article shows promise and promotion might motivate the candidate to greater heights." It's always hard to turn someone down who hasn't made it and never will. How do you keep them motivated? You know what, you can't. Oh well, now out of our hands, over to the committee.

I headed for the faculty club hoping to get in and out before Harv's arrival. I was only half finished my jug of beer when Harv's shadow covered the table. He draped his jacket over the chair beside me and slumped into the remaining one. Without hesitation he asked how his buddy made out. I told him that rules of confidentiality sealed my lips. He shook his head, scowled and muttered, "It's so hard to have creativity and innovation recognized by the entrenched establishment." He pointed out he had read the recent paper and said it's first rate and path breaking. I broke my silence and said it barely made a third rate journal. That didn't faze Harv a bit. He again pointed out that the established journals too suffer from creative myopia.

Episode

Group Think

DOUBLE YOUR PLEASURE, double your fun, do it
with two or more instead of just one.

I am involved in a group research project with two senior
colleagues of our department. On a personal level we have
little in common but on the research front we each bring
something to the table that makes us stronger as a group.
They are both salt of the earth types, committed to the pur-
ist of academic pursuits. One has a chair and the other is
likely to get his own chair in the near future. The dean almost
has the financing together to make it a reality. He better
because we know of at least two other universities that have
their sights set on attracting him with a well funded chair.

How did I get into such an august group? The research
project we are engaged in requires access to the inner
sanctum of some major organizations. Through a tie to a
couple of former students that I had befriended during
some grade difficulties I was able to call in a few favour

chits and gain entry. It's not that I don't contribute more to our research pursuits, I just haven't climbed to the highest rung of the academic ladder. No doubt because I keep getting distracted by other interests or as I like to claim, a wide range of eclectic tastes. When I'm feeling expansive I like to think of myself as a latter day Renaissance man. You may not be surprised to learn that is not a view shared by one and all. I had a supervisor during graduate student days who unkindly cut me with the term dilettante. Not the kind of reputation to help a young scholar through graduate school.

The remaining members of the team are slaves. Not in name of course, just in how they are treated and what they are asked to do. They are officially called graduate students. We have attracted one of each gender. It was easy enough to do since we have one of the largest research grants in our faculty. They get to do all the detail work and number grinding analysis. In return we put their names at the end of research papers and pay them an almost livable stipend.

Harv and some of my other faculty club soul mates sometimes raise an eyebrow over the presence of a female in our research group. They might have had cause to in my earlier career but no longer. Let's just say I'm not up to it these days. Of course the young lassie and I have never been out of town together. I'm sure neither of my two sexually correct colleagues would entertain the notion of reclining with the sweet, clear skinned, blue eyed and robust young delight. And if they did I'd be more surprised than if I won a Nobel Prize. I'm less sure about the male grad student of our group. I notice he and blue eyes have been finding excuses for more research trips together. I prefer to accept the upfront work argument and if there is more I don't want to know.

Our research group met this week. We once tried to meet every week but that didn't last long. We decided we didn't like each other that much and it took up the productive part of an afternoon and worse for me cut into my drinking time at the faculty club. There was a proposal to meet in the evening which I didn't like because I'd have to leave the faculty club early and if I was true to the team show up sober. Fortunately, I didn't have to say anything. One of our group has a couple of school age kids and is not allowed out at night unless on a family errand. Most likely ferrying the kids to or from some educational or health conscious pursuit. Now we meet as needed which seems to work out to about once every two weeks. We do have a policy to not let more than three weeks go by without a get together.

A team approach is certainly how research is done now. The day of the sole practitioner toiling in search of the truth is interred in the dinosaur museum. The risks of playing the Lone Ranger on the research frontier are too great. The proper matching of skills will usually give more bang for the research buck.

One can try to play the role of grand theoretician, which if done successfully will put you at the pinnacle of the academic pecking order, but that is even riskier. To pull together disparate scraps of data and musings and come up with something truly original is no mean feat. One that is well beyond my capabilities and ambition and most relevant, energy level.

The use of a team approach to research very much adds an organizational and managerial dimension to the enterprise. Something I'm rather good at when I put my mind to it. Somehow the group has to sort out the design of the research, figure out where and how to collect the data, what kind of analysis will be done and who by and in the end make sure the work is written up and presented at conferences and published in the top academic journals. And of course write and send in the obligatory reports to the granting agencies more or less on time. The group gives me free rein to see the necessary gets done by someone close enough to the deadline that we get to live another day.

Nothing underlines the businesslike reality of research more than the revenue generating function of grant application. Without revenue the type and level of research possible soon shrinks into insignificance. And nothing is so uninteresting and neglected as research tagged insignificant.

Today's meeting was all about revenue generation. If we are to continue with our research we will soon be in need of a cash infusion. And if we are to stay together as a group it will need to be very large indeed. Today we have to decide on the two main activities. What is the topic and who will write the proposal. The first carries prestige and the latter is grunt work. I sit on the sidelines with the grad students while my two esteemed colleagues have a tussle over the topic. They seem to get a testosterone rush from claiming at conferences that the work is basically their idea. I'm happy to go along to get along and as long as we get the money I claim success. As for the grad students, no one would listen to them anyway.

Today's dispute was quickly settled by reference to the granting agency's guidelines for the coming year. It would only support one of the two topics raised. Who would prepare the proposal was easy. As always, me the writing and the grad students the leg work on references and such uninteresting trivia.

I did a quick calculation on a ballpark amount of cash we

would need and doubled it. Everyone knows that reviewers think it is their job to suggest cuts to whatever you ask for. One of the key characteristics of successful grant grubbing is to know by how much to inflate the request so you get the amount you want.

I once reviewed a proposal and suggested the researcher should be given more than he asked for. I thought the topic was a good one but a decent job would require more than the requested amount. I no longer find my nights occupied with reviewing research proposals from that granting agency.

The final topic before ending the meeting was who we would suggest as reviewers. That meant coming up with friends and supposed experts who would tell loving lies about our expertise and dedication to actually do what we said we would do. It's funny how the vagaries of life and changes in the research scene set investigators off in directions they had not originally contemplated. Only later does one confront how to put together a tortured tale that explains how what you really did fits in with what you said you would do. Many are the paths to truth and new insights under the guise of research.

9

Episode

A Leader for the Unleadable

NEW DEAN TIME. How do I know? The faculty web site says so and that's the same as getting it on tablets delivered by a hippy dude called Moses. It used to be we got pieces of paper stuck in our cubby-hole mail boxes called memos that announced all news fit to print _ or not. Not anymore. Now it's on the computer. At least it's eliminated a lot of clutter from errant memos misdirected in the general direction of the rubbish bin. I never showed such a blatant lack of respect. I always transported them back to my office and floated them around the room as paper airplanes. I no longer have raw material for aeronautical construction.

Why do we need a new dean? Now that question bears the label of imponderable. Well, not at a simple level of course. The faculty organization chart has a box for one. And eventually it will be noticed at certain meetings that our lonely group of scholars lacks representation. But why do we really need a dean in a functional sense? Back to imponderable.

Meetings comes first to mind. It's more efficient to appoint one person to attend the plethora of meetings that is the bitter complaint of everyone inside our hallowed halls. It sends chills up my spine if the dean quit attending meetings and reallocated them among the rest of us miscreants.

The most important meetings are the butt covering ones. The ones where the dean girds for battle and rides forth to ensure our faculty gets a fair whack of the pies that matter. The most important is the cash pie. That pie determines the size of our empire. It allows us to keep and attract the type of colleagues we can get along with. And when one escapes over the moat we can sally forth to search out a replacement.

Success in garnering a large slice of the cash pie also supports our quality of life. This includes the all important travel money to get us out of town and off to the finer world capitals or resorts that the brainy among us select for annual academic meetings. It's obligatory to attend such meetings for periodic one-upmanship drinking sessions to find out who among our graduate school buddies has landed the most goodies lately. And on occasion one gets lucky. No, I won't go into depth on that topic.

And of course included in the list is cash to support the people that brighten my day and make it easier to come to work. Top of the list is Bambi, the Star of our department. And also in the support category are the tools and trinkets of the trade like computers, fax machines, papers, pencils, paper clips and such.

So now that I look at the harsh reality in the cruel light of day maybe we better get on with the job and find a dean. And as happens so often in life the reason is cash. Not only cash from the coffers of academia but someone who has the skills to find cheques in the world beyond the moat . It is now an accepted fact that the meager funds provided by the university no longer offer the life style we know we deserve. We need a real hunter to catch the quarry, bring it home, clean it, cook it and clean up afterwards. No longer the great academic leader that was once the ideal. Now it's someone with the business connections of a venture capitalist, the networking finesse of a web administrator and the cunning of a snake oil salesman.

Of course we do have to be careful in trampling on tradition. A dean is party to many decisions that strike to the heart of all we hold dear. We wouldn't want the wrong people promoted or granted tenure because the dean is unaware of, or insensitive to all matters that lie at the heart of our craft.

We also wouldn't want the wrong sorts of innovations shuffled through the back door. I heard a story where a dean brought in from something like a washing machine company of all places put up an In and Out board. You had to advertise to all the world whether you were In or Out and if not In, explain where you were. Another horrific example is a careless selection committee appointed a management consultant. His first innovation was individual business plans with hard measurable objectives that were to be reported on semi-annually. I'm overjoyed to say both attempts were abject failures. The challenge was met in the same way in both cases. Ignored until they went away, along with the ill-placed selection.

When the time comes to actually examine a potential list of candidates for an administrative position like a dean we confront an academic catch-22. Anyone you think you would want in the position wouldn't be caught dead playing dean. But anyone who openly seeks the position is usually the last person in the world you would appoint. A true conundrum.

Another question that always comes up at dean appointment time is internal versus external candidate. Appointing a known quantity means everyone has a better idea of skeletons in closets and where the bodies are hid. You are less likely to have your life disrupted. Of course there is no guarantee. No dean is more reviled than the trusted former colleague who wants to make a reputation by shaking up the place. Most don't try, or at least not for long.

If someone gets the foolish notion that there is a need for new blood and a shake-up it can make for a period of disruption until the candidate is trained in the ways of your institution or the dean becomes an ex-dean. Too often it is forgotten that the outsiders lack a group of cronies who will help get things done. The external dean will not have a set of favours to call in. And without coin of the realm bankruptcy looms, followed soon by a silent departure.

At the end of the day no matter who is appointed the dean will fall out of favour. At some point decisions must be made with limited resources. Funding requests will be turned down, salary demands ignored. The wrong people will be promoted, or not. The halls will ring with plaintiff's murmurs of the dean's failure to live up to expectations. It will be noticed that the appointee isn't ten feet tall after all but more like four foot, six. Questions will be raised how such a disastrous appointment could be made and fingers pointed at the myopic selection committee.

Now the wheel has turned full circle we are back to hunting down a new dean. So let loose the search dogs. The first step follows the grand academic tradition for making virtually all decisions. Strike a committee. As in all similar circumstances you'll find me in a dark corner at the faculty club sharing suds and wisdom with Harv. I will not be party to a process that is guaranteed to end badly and besmirch my reputation.

10

Episode

To Arms, To Arms, The Enemy's at the Gates, No It's Us

A STRIKE. AT this very minute a vote will decide if we hit the bricks. I can't believe it. It can't happen. At least not to me.

Chirst, we're not labourers. We don't go out and dig and hammer. There isn't a person in this place that doesn't have clean fingernails. How could we arrive at such a sorry state?

When the prospect of a union was first broached I laughed it off as the twisted response of a few deranged faculty members whose intellectual and political skills weren't up to shuffling them through the ranks like well mannered academics. As usual in such practical ways of the world the bell rang - Tilt. The organizers collected the necessary signatures to hold a vote. I didn't attend the meeting and of course didn't vote. I gather I was part of the majority in not attending even if my views were not part of the majority that voted.

I woke in a daze one morning and not for the usual reason of the previous evening's excess but more the surprise that we had a union. Once again, confirmation of what every union organizer and revolutionary knows, a well organized minority can rule the rabble majority any day of the week.

I heard one could opt out of the union if you filled in a frightening array of forms and carried an approving signature from some important person like your mother, priest, or even a dean. But in my case and I'm sure others of a similar ilk, sloth and inertia leapt to the fore and nothing was done. There is little point in opting out anyway because dues are still deducted from one's monthly pittance and you're bound by the negotiated contract like any dues paying member.

Much to the surprise of many, including skeptics and myself, the union received praise that surpassed the most optimistic predictions for the first couple of years. They took credit for increases in salaries and improved benefits beyond experience and expectation. What few noticed, except maybe the union, is we enjoyed a time of bounty. The government, our major source of funds heaped more largesse upon the university than had ever been their custom. Come negotiation time the administration readily passed on the gain to us in the trenches. The tide raises all boats.

As too often happens in economic matters good times do not roll forever. The fare laid before us by the union began to take on the flavour of a thin and tasteless gruel. The less grateful among us started to raise uncommon business like questions about getting a return on our union dues. Our union leaders acquired the title, Lords of the Manor. They took our dues to pay themselves lavish honorariums, received reduced teaching loads, if any, and of course claimed a life of grim toil on behalf of their overworked and exploited colleagues to even consider serious research. Of course they could bear this great sacrifice to their professional fulfillment and career advancement when they saw the benefits heaped upon the huddled, toiling masses.

But something must now be done. The masses had gone soft and the time had come to strengthen their backbone. And, oh yes, bring to the fore the benefits and unquestioned relevance of the union. The most recent insult was a meager wage offer. No siree Bob, we weren't going to take it anymore. As honourable women and men of principle we must stand together. The administration gave us no alternative but to hit the bricks. That's right - STRIKE.

My first reaction was ridicule. Who would even notice if we went on strike. And more important, what about getting paid. As so often happens in such confrontations the perpetrators try to convince everyone that it is not about the money. That of course confirms that it sure as hell is about the money.

Once again, my predictive powers failed. Harv came into the faculty club waving a piece of paper. "It's on," he shouted, much too loud for the sepulcher atmosphere of the faculty club. I didn't have to ask and slumped further into my chair. Harv grabbed my hand and tried to pull me erect. When I resisted he said there was no time to lose. We had to make our strike placards and sign up for picket duty. When I confessed that I didn't think I'd join the strike he went over to the bar and returned with a full and large jug. I could see that I was to be plied with the time honored strike lubricant _ booze.

It worked. Here I am marching back and forth like a Russian border guard toting an oversized square of cardboard tacked onto an abandoned hockey stick. I ran out of black paint so the scrawled message in red and black reads – 'Slaves No More, Strike for a Living Wage.' I wish I had Harv's creativity – 'Satanic Sweatshop No More, On Strike for Human Rights.'

I thought all we had to do was march back and forth to support the cause and get our trifling strike pay. About ten per cent of our regular pay as I calculated it. That is if we ever collect. I had no idea that aggression would invade my day.

We had all of the roads blocked into the university but each day a phantom biker challenged us. He would tear across the field on his mountain bike beyond our reach ringing his bell and cackling, "Get to work you worthless deadbeats." Our inability to stop him finally sent one of our number demented who brought in his kid's BB gun. When the biker appeared the crazed picketer opened fire. Recognizing a change in rules the biker rose in his seat to lengthen the distance from us. Bad idea. He took one right up the butt. Harv immediately stepped in and relieved the Rifleman of his weapon. Most of us thought it bad form to escalate firearms into the conflict. But it was effective. No more biker after that day. No more firearms either since Harv held onto the gun until the strike ended.

The conflict escalated the day the president's car pulled up to our post and all of my fellow marchers rushed to block her exit. Fortunately, at that exact moment I found myself at the opposite end of the picket line. I prayed I might turn myself into a puff of smoke and blow away. No such luck. My next best refuge was a Port-A-Potty. You know, one of those foul green sheds that border construction sights. I took a deep breath and dived inside. I could peek through a hole in the door and take in the outside world. It gave me a ringside view of an assault on a picket by the president's car. As the car turned to flee the scene a picket rushed over to give the president some personal advice. Something along the lines of, "fucking anti-intellectual, ball-less lackey of the capitalist exploiters." Unfortunately, at that very same moment the president's car took an escape route across the foot of the picket. Soon great cries of assault, legal charges and law suits filled the air. By then only the whiff of exhaust identified the president's appearance.

Inside the putrid refuge my breath gave out at the exact moment the president's car departed. I returned blue faced to the picket line to confront a red-faced Harv. He informed me there would be no more dereliction of duty and deserters could meet a harsh fate. He didn't actually say shot but his demeanor indicated it had been a consideration and he still held onto the BB gun.

I might have acted differently at my next confrontation if it hadn't followed so close upon Harv's fearful threat. I promised to strengthen my resolve and marched toward the barricade, actually a line drawn on the pavement. In my darker moments I tried to lift my spirits by likening the barricade and our cause to Les Miserables. I no doubt would have found the fantasy easier if I'd had a bucket of real spirits on hand.

They say timing is everything. I know that because I'm so good at bad timing. I joined the ranks on the line at the same instant as Bambi, driving her pink Volkswagen convertible arrived. Top down of course. Being a brisk day she warded off the chill in a soft angora sweater of the same colour as the car. I leaned into the car, my mouth short circuited my brain and I announced, "Nice headlights."

She blushed, slapped my hand and replied, "Naughty."

"On the car of course," as I compounded my ill mannered comment.

She promised I'd be forgiven if I let her pass. When I refused she went into a pout and cancelled all our coffee dates for the rest of the millennium. I told her the success of our strike depended on not letting people continue with their work. She said her presence had nothing to do with work. She merely wanted to retrieve her favorite lipstick from a desk drawer in her office. I restored some semblance of respect and favour when I promised to do the retrieving for her.

The strike carried on somewhere between a week and forever. Harv told me a week. The inner me confirmed forever. We started on a Monday and by Thursday I had lost all track of time and reality. I even filled in on one night shift. I considered manning the line in the middle of the night on the other side of barmy. Harv said we couldn't allow any scabs sneaking in in the middle of the night to check e-mail or worse, work on a paper. I found myself standing around an old barrel with a blazing fire that we fed with the most recent offer from the administration. The size of our midnight tribe grew with the addition of the graduate student union executive bearing gifts in the form of hot dogs to roast over the fire and a large thermos of coffee. The best part was the bottle of rum they brought to fortify the coffee.

There was just enough left in the rum bottle to share a dollop with Harv when he arrived for the morning shift. When I told him the origins of the bottle and the generosity of the graduate students he said we'd have ample opportunity to pay them back. They too had negotiations coming up later in the year that would likely lead to a strike and would be looking for support. I made a note to check on the likely date to prepare in advance to be on a plane to elsewhere or home bound with a deadly and highly communicable disease.

When the strike entered a second week I made a pledge to not shave until it ended. Kind of like a hockey player as the first puck was about to drop for the playoffs. I also thought of not changing my shorts and socks for the same reason but decided that might be cruel punishment to my fellow brick pacers. Later that day we heard the administration had come forth with a new offer that the union troika agreed to put to a ballot by the membership.

The graduate students must have given them several bottles of rum because I don't think that upon cold and sober reflection the troika would have allowed a vote. They did sober up in time to send out a directive to reject the offer. But this time everyone showed up to vote, not just their phalanx of hard core supporters. An overwhelming majority voted to end the strike. I rushed home to shave and treat myself to the bottom half of my most venerable bottle of single malt.

The next day I arrived at the office later than usual. I had to wait for the stores to open so I could make a few high priority purchases. I needed peace offerings for Bambi to solidify future coffee dates. I picked up a cashmere sweater in what I hoped was the right shade of pink and the obligatory one size too small. For immediate consumption I visited a special local shop called Repairs. No, it's not for cars or home renovation, it carries special gifts to put damaged relationships back on track. They specialize in bouquets of exotic flowers and chocolate truffles that are more expensive than the real kind French pigs find under trees. It all worked and my vicarious sex life is back on track.

I found Harv at the faculty club for a strike post mortem. He was resigned to the end of his days of glory as a group leader at the barricades. He claimed us academics deserved a downtrodden fate since we lacked the gonads to stand up for our rights. I wondered, but didn't say if Harv had any idea how lucky he was, even if stalled as an Associate Professor. As far as I could tell where else could Harv collect a regular cheque for showing up a few times a week to send a group of undergraduates to dreamland? As for myself, I have an emergency plan that will whisk me out of harms way and far from the picket line if another such disaster looms on the horizon. No, I'm not revealing anything. It is the one real secret I will never divulge. Well, maybe to Bambi if she crooks her little finger and asks.

Episode

Publish or Perish, the Thought

PUBLISH OR PERISH. Now there's a thought that cools the cockles o' me heart. I don't think I made the connection when I got into this racket. Actually, I'm not sure how much thinking I did do. I doubt that alone makes me unusual. How much thinking, planning and foresight does anyone put into career decisions? Like marriage and most other life altering events I'm of the view that action takes place at the level of the visceral. What weight to place on the pecuniary versus social standing versus the work of a profession. Does a person become a doctor for the money? Or is it the prestige of answering the 'What do you do,' question with the response, 'I am a doctor.' Or the even more heavily weighted 'I am a physician.' Or is the profession adopted because of an overwhelming need to do good and save the sick, ill and downtrodden.

Maybe some people do but if so I don't know them and rarely enter into that kind of conversation. I'm inclined to think a direction is followed where there is maximum return for minimum effort. A little casual empiricism in my own work world finds overwhelming support for that hypothesis.

My attraction to enter the Crypt of Academe had a lot to do with my anti-social bent. Greta Garbo and I must share a common ancient relative. I too just, 'vant to be alone'. I thought by choosing an academic career I could keep myself amused in the solitude of my office solving puzzles of my own choosing and on my own schedule. It took me some time to fully appreciate that gaining entry into the hallowed halls would require placing the results of my puzzle solving on public display. I would have to devote no small amount of effort to the publishing game if I wanted to maintain any self-respect, to say nothing of my job.

Now the publishing game is no simple task. One does not just sit down one day, writing instrument at hand, once upon a time a pen or pencil, now more likely a computer and transfer a few random thoughts to paper and stick the results in an envelope for delivery to the editor of what is called a learned journal. No, no, no! It doesn't work that way, not one little bit.

A variety of outlets for publishing are available in the academic world. There are textbooks, scholarly works on arcane topics, the collected results of conferences and compendiums where some so called leader in the field asks friends to contribute a paper to advance knowledge on a subject of crucial importance to the welfare of humanity. These are all relevant and important entrants in the publishing game but the gold standard is publication in the most reputed peer reviewed journals of one's chosen field of endeavor. Having an avaricious bent I will confine my comments to the gold standard.

Ante for the game is an idea. Now it can't be just any idea but an idea no one has thought of before. Or at least an idea where if you paint it a different shade of blue people will think it's new. After all, ours is a creative field of endeavour and how can you look creative regurgitating the familiar? The bigger the idea the better of course. And if it is big enough you can dine off that idea for the rest of your career. And in the case of true genius it may launch an entire academic industry that transits the centuries. But there are few among us who will reach the heights of Newton, Einstein, Pasteur or Shakespeare.

At the end of the day most, admittedly not all, academic writing is more a fractional turn of the prism to cast light at a different angle that captures a change in hue. The writer has a choice of turning the idea into a theoretical article or an empirical one. The theoretical alternative is a set of ideas to explain something and carries a heavier burden of success. An empirical article means data and numbers and is more likely to appear in print. Even if your ideas are borrowed and familiar your numbers will be different than anyone else's. You are no doubt not surprised to learn that I travel in the empirical realm.

At this time I won't lead you through the agony of the research process _ idea, design, data collection, analysis and our topic of today, write-up. It looks like a nice simple process where the ducks of the A, B, Cs are all in a row. It never works like that but at some time you must call a halt and get on with the agony of getting into print.

I'm not a natural at the writing game and I suspect that's typical of most Crypt dwellers. Otherwise, why wouldn't we be earning our daily crust in the field of fiction and literature? The irony is our fame and livelihood depends on a talent that is not at the top of the list of our more positive attributes.

I have a further personal problem. When the time has come to get down to writing I know the results. I know the answer to the problem that started us down the research path. It may not and probably is not the answer I was looking for at the outset but the data is in. I get my jollies out of finding something unknown, not grinding on the computer to present the answer in the best light possible.

I try to save my non-classroom days for writing. Like many of my brethren I think proper writing requires long blocks of uninterrupted time to gather one's thoughts and warm to the task. I try to warm up as if I were to engage in some form of athletic endeavour. I know how to warm up for a work-out. I ride the exercise bike or trot gently on a treadmill. To warm up for writing I once read light humour but that was in pre-computer days. Now I Google around the internet through the usual male subjects _ sex, booze and sports. Harv tells me it has nothing to do with warming up and everything to do with avoidance behaviour. When confronted by Harv I defend my good name with great vigor but in the quiet of my own study I know he's right.

I eventually get down to the task. I have to. I know you can buy software that helps write screen plays and novels but so far I've not encountered such a boon for academic toil. I usually start with what's known, the results. No sense starting with the hard part which is some 'creative' explanation about the source of these unexpected results. It's not as though you're entirely on your own since there is a formula for our kind of writing which does have a certain rationale but makes for a less than riveting story. Ergo, the reason for the academic - boring link in the world of the written world. I once asked an editor if it would be possible to submit an article that contained a modicum of humour. The editor was not amused.

An article starts with an Introduction that warns the reader what it is you're about, thereby giving said person a chance for an early escape. Since it is well known that there is nothing new under the sun one must acknowledge the fact. This is done in a section called Literature Review. It is a chance to pay homage to all those who have gone before. This should be done in a 'yes but' fashion. On the one hand you acknowledge the great contributions of the pioneers who toiled before in the untilled fields making ready for those of us to have an easier life. On the other hand one points out that despite their best efforts there are still gaps and questions of deep importance begging, nay crying for resolution. After all, why the hell are you wasting the readers' time if something has already been done? The end point of the section is the rationale for the study you're about to describe.

In performing the literature review there are certain rules that if not followed make for quick and easy rejection by editors. Editors have a constant problem of demand vastly exceeding supply. Too many manuscripts, too few journal slots. Any chance for a quick rejection is leaped upon as fox upon a lame rabbit. One is to acknowledge the great and the good. To not do so is bad manners and evidence of a poor education. One may then move on to more strategic inclusion. The first is your own work. For one thing it boosts your citation index which may be used as evidence for, or against you, at certain critical career junctures like tenure and promotion. And as my Granny used to say, "If you won't blow your own horn, who will." I would also suggest that you try and fit in references to the work of friends. If you don't you may have trouble finding suitable drinking companions at your next conference. Or worse, someone to tell loving lies in references for promotion and grant applications.

The research design and analysis of results follow next. Both are of a technical nature and dead boring to all but the cognoscenti of the field of study. I will say no more about them. Although they can lead to bitter warfare between proponents of opposing views.

I can't prove it but am of the opinion that the vast majority of readers of such material leap past these sections to the main interest of the article, the results. In a just and fair world the results would clearly favour the hypotheses, or not. Preferably the former from the investigator's point of view. The researcher's digestion suffers when the results are indeterminate, neither clearly for, nor clearly against. You may think creativity comes to the fore at the inception of the research, in coming up with the idea and then the design. Oh ye of little clue. I should know because I've had a great deal of practice. My usual strategy is to put a positive spin on such results and point out how they reveal fruitful lines of research previously unknown to the ken of humankind.

. Up to this point one is expected to stick to the canons of science and operate within a tightly constructed theoretical framework and not stray out of sight of the results. But the final section allows one to leap off the cliff of speculation in a full flight of fantasy. As Harv says, let loose with the purple prose and damn the hyperbole. It is my favorite section. By the time I get to it I'm usually numb and have trouble remembering the intended destination in this voyage of discovery. When the light goes on to let loose with the most wondrous of speculations I experience an almost other worldly testosterone rush.

One writing of a paper is never enough. Several drafts are obligatory to produce a finally honed product. After all, who would want the embarrassment of a rejoinder, "Obviously a first draft, let me see it again when you have a final draft." At such time as you think the final draft stage has arrived is the time to reveal your creation to valued colleagues. By valued I mean those who will provide useful but not soul destroying feedback. I belong to a network that circulates our papers with an unspoken understanding of what is expected.

When the feedback is collected another round of rewrites is necessary. How many you ask? There is no hard and fast rule. I do it until I can't stand the sound, sight or smell of the paper anymore. You then stuff the fruits of your labour into an envelope and off it goes on a wing and a prayer to the journal of choice.

Your future is now in the hands of a journal editor and three anonymous reviewers. Here we have one of the foundations of the academic world. The blind review. It is thought that the benefit of anonymity will ensure a full and fair evaluation of your masterpiece that you hope will vault you into the foremost ranks of your profession. Or at least help support a boost in salary and prevent a boost in teaching load.

Just when you think your submission was lost in the ether and are on the verge of reaching for the phone or e-mail to enquire about the status of much sweat and tears a large brown envelope appears in your mailbox. You know what it is without looking at any postmark. Should I retreat to the sanctuary of my office and divulge the contents in private. Should I even look at it today? Maybe first thing in the morning after a good night's sleep. Maybe in the company of a good friend like Harv. Or ask Bambi to read it first so she can let you down gently if it's bad news. I nearly always opt for the sanctuary of my office. No sense exposing my failure to those near and dear if such is the result.

The best result would be acceptance without revisions. That has never happened to me, nor to anyone I know of on the face of this earth. I am more familiar with a letter of outright rejection, no chance for revisions. And from time to time I get a letter asking for revisions according to reviewers' comments and resubmission. I'm never sure if the latter isn't the worst of all possible outcomes. It means more work and giving in to reviewers' opinions that you likely think came from a mentally challenged chimp, if that comment isn't too politically incorrect, re: chimps. But of course I give in, supplicate, make the changes, send off the revised article and wait another interminable period for a response. What else can one do, after all, isn't the name of the game, Publish or Perish?

The reviewers are meant to be anonymous but I always play the Guess Who game. Just who did make those inane and career destroying comments? I keep a list of certain candidates and a second one of most likely candidates. Who knows when I may get a chance to repay their 'compliment' with a review of one of their articles?

A second submission is much like the first with the results communicated in a large brown envelope. Again one hopes for acceptance without revisions but there are no guarantees and I have seen a thank you but not up to our standards for an original contribution. That means a quick exit to join Harv and this time for an extra jug of soul soothing brew. More often it is publish if I will again supplicate to a final round of revisions. Once I was asked for a third resubmission with no guarantee of publication. I developed an entirely new hit list for that editor and the one reviewer of the three that I was certain I could identify.

When the final congratulatory letter of acceptance is to hand I become uncontrollably joyous and make a great cheerful din around the department. It also gives me a chance to hoist Bambi in a great bear hug. It's easy to pass that off as the enthusiasm of success instead of off the rails sexual harassment. When my testosterone settles back to near normal I sprint to the faculty club to share my glory with Harv and whoever else is at the table. As they raise their glass in congratulations I pass it off as a simple daily event with the outcome never in doubt. Once again I didn't perish and live to publish another day.

12

Episode

New Blood

THE HIRING GAME is on. That's right, an injection of new blood for our department. The powers that be have given the purse a shake and enough money came flooding out to give us the go ahead to add a fresh young face to our department. They didn't even specify the sex, colour or religious preference of likely candidates. Just the old and I thought forgotten homily to go forth and carry back the best available newly minted Ph D.

Loud hosannas normally rattle the halls at the prospect of a new hire. Not unlike that of a new offspring on the way. Once the hosannas recede to a murmur the skirmishes begin. No department is a homogeneous group but more a mish mash of special and often widely divergent specialties, each one convinced without reservation that the new addition should be one of them. For a period of time the political knives come out and honed to a fine edge. At some point we affect a resolution, usually imposed from the outside.

Sometimes by the department chair who can no longer abide the squabbling and special pleas. The last time the dean did it by informing us that if we didn't cast aside our childish bickering he would banish us from the playground and give our hiring ball to a more mature group that knew how to play nice.

The charge of locating and hiring the best available may seem simple on first blush. Unfortunately, best is a word that translates into many and varied meanings if you traverse the tortured trail into the neighbourhood of concrete criteria that is descriptive of an actual human being. In the academic world we have learned to side step such pitfalls. Instead we rely on a bucket of secondary criteria and thereby pass the buck elsewhere.

Best becomes coterminous with reputation. The reputation of graduate school, reputation of thesis supervisor and if available any publications the candidate has been able to attach his or her name to in reputable journals. I think the simplicity and safety of it all now becomes self-evident. If the candidate is a bust the blame can be placed on others. After all we went to the best for their best.

Among the elite the process begins by canvassing the brethren to enquire if their pipeline contains any likely candidates. The process may include direct contact with the heralded members of the profession to see if they will send any of their ingénues our way. A sort of unofficial incest exists in the academic community as the more promising students are cycled amongst an inner group who think their students are worthy of trading back and forth to each other to retain a tight control of the intellectual sperm bank. It is not uncommon to learn that a renowned supervisor has blocked a student moving to an institution his or her mentor thinks of as inferior. The supervisor would be of the opinion that years of molding the plasticene mind of a young person into something of refined intellect that will make major contributions to the knowledge of the world and thereby further enhance the reputation of their supervisor will not be thwarted by casting the seed upon barren and infertile soil. It is always with great pride that academic leaders like to pontificate when a weighty issue comes up with such phrases as: "Ah yes, I have a student working on that problem." Or, as the leading new lights are recognized and rewarded: "Ah yes, one of my former students you know." With an addendum along the lines of, "Who has started a very promising career at" (the reader may insert the name of their favorite institution of renown).

Once the initial list of likely candidates has been obtained from annual meetings and selected supervisors the committee must winnow it down to a select few. There may be a few applicants who responded to the obligatory ad in the usual academic outlets but as with most unsolicited mail, disposal proves easy. Once the short list is agreed upon the heavy lifting of the recruiting process begins in earnest.

We now turn to candidate examination, up close and personal. This is done by what is sometimes called a dog and pony show. It is sort of an attempt at an in-depth search inside the candidate to check out not only the molars but their very soul to evaluate the presence of a life long commitment to the rigors of our profession. The ideal is someone who is fully infused with an academic career as a calling. Not as merely a job with a light work load that includes a good salary. That is why one of my now long gone former mentors thought that academics shouldn't be paid too much because they'll only sign on for the money and not the calling. I won't comment on his era but as for mine I have no doubts that he would be sorely disillusioned.

The dog and pony show involves an exhausting round of an onstage live performance, personal grilling and tests of social graces. The candidate is cycled through a continuous revolution of all department members and a few non-department members who are dragooned into participating for their independent evaluation. My own memory of the experience was an assault of the same questions repeated over and over. I soon decided that what I needed was a recording that I could turn on as soon as I walked through an office door. At some point the day comes to an end and so too the questions. The live performance where the candidate presents their thesis to the assembly of the department usually winds up the day.

Institutions acquire a reputation on how they treat recruiting candidates at presentation. At one time we relished the rigour of our incisive and 'honest' questioning. That is until we were informed from various sources that never had there been such a bunch of precious prats whose only interest was personal self-aggrandizement through the skewering of defenseless souls. We have now reformed. A clear inability to attract candidates from any source helped greatly in our rehabilitation.

By now the rumour mill is fully operational and many minds are made up. Others remain open which means they have no opinion and are not likely to have one. We know who they are because the latest news is their news. If the word is positive the evening meal will be a joyous affair as we try to impress the candidate with what good company we are. If the word is negative the evening meal has all the joy of banqueting with Macbeth and is soon over.

After all the candidates have passed through our portals the selection committee gathers the written evaluation forms. These include numerical estimates beside a variety of criteria and opportunities for individual comments. The latter vary from cruel and caustic to special pleadings that would make a mother blush. Such comments may be traced to a special relationship between the writer and the candidate's supervisor or the candidate is an advocate of the writer's own pet theory. It is presumed the numerical evidence is the precursor to any conclusion about the candidate. I'm of the view that a from the gut conclusion informs the numbers.

We carefully read the evaluation forms, reflect on our own personal experience with the candidates and allow that reason and evidence must be relied upon for such an important decision. While all nodding sagely and bowing to the first commandment of selection we go with our guts. I know I do but only after I've assembled what looks like a rational argument from the available evidence.

Once a preferred candidate is selected we turn the final stage over to the dean. This is not by preference since few academics trust a dean with anything important but must be done according to university rules. It is the dean who makes the formal offer that includes salary, teaching load and other benefits. The dean must balance a fine point of offering enough to attract likely candidates without going overboard and disrupting the department salary structure. That means getting the old lags like me cranky because a newly minted Ph D will be making almost as much as they do and teaching fewer courses. When the dean announces the deal is done it is over.

Much is left before final consummation but it is now the senior administrators who must take over. Little problems creep in like the candidate changing their mind at the last minute. Read better offer from better place. Shows up and makes unreasonable demands like the corner office I've had my eye on for eons. Or worst of all, and this has happened, moves in on Bambi, my prime source of departmental solace. Now that is unforgivable. It's much worse even than having this newbie join an opposing political group in the department.

I try to meet the candidate as soon as possible after arrival, preferably on the first day under the guise of a guided tour of the faculty club and introductions to the 'right' people. I think it's important that any new candidate learns what is 'right' and who is 'right' so they will become a proper fit in the department.

13

Episode

Come the Seventh Thou Shall Rest

IF GOD, WHY not me? I'm sure the first academic said something like that when asked to justify taking off every seventh year. Nowadays, one hears arguments more along the lines of need for reflection, renewal or concentrated time to start or complete a research project of world altering importance. Not unlike the summer siesta between the end of classes in spring and recommencement in September. In all cases such fallow time is absolutely and without argument necessary because of the soul destroying and mind numbing toil of the regular term due to teaching, professional demands and an out of control research program.

Every university that I know of and certainly any I would consider for a position includes a sabbatical leave as part of the academic employment contract. Of course it's not available to all dwellers of the Crypt but only those of exalted academic status. The unannointed labouring classes who tend to the stroking of the academic psyche get the usual two to six weeks of common holidays, kind of like the rest of the toiling masses beyond the moat of the Crypt.

Of course the right to swan off in the seventh year isn't just handed to you. A person must be a member in good standing. You know, fully paid dues at the faculty club and not annoyed anyone of importance who might be in a position to sign the appropriate approval papers.

The appropriate application papers are the starting point to set off on the sabbatical journey. They are meant to detail how you and the university will benefit from your time apart. In other words what the hell will you be up to during that year away? It tells how you will benefit professionally, maybe even personally and on occasion I've seen suggestions of spiritual revival. The most recent came from a dude in Psychology who wanted to search his inner soul in some ashram in India and cast out a few demons. His justifications included throwing back the frontiers of comparative psychology and ground breaking new therapies in clinical treatments, especially people suffering from drug addiction. I'm not sure what he did, or if he ever made it to India but I did see him on his return in a long white dress with a year's growth of hair on face and head and a rather emaciated look as he leaned on an ever present crooked stick. From what I hear he must be continuing his drug research because his mail is sent to a famous substance abuse rehabilitation center.

Location, location, location is almost as important for sabbaticals as real estate. For some of us even ahead of what we claim we'll do. Some universities try to make it mandatory to take a sabbatical at other than a home institution. After all, what kind of renewal is going to take place if you stay home, go into the same office, talk the same boring shop with the same colleagues and drink beer with the same cronies? What's different? Very little bar the demands of classroom performance. However, when the decision drops to the bottom line I've never known anyone denied a sabbatical because they wanted to stay in the same locale. And those who do are usually smart enough to avoid the office. Who needs the slings and arrows from colleagues who must continue their toil in the classroom trenches?

Time away does not always return the expected rewards. I remember the bankruptcy of another colleague who truly wanted a major change and decamped for Paris. I hated him for his good fortune. Turned out he had never been beyond the shores of our fabled land and didn't speak the language, nor did he include language instruction in his preparation. His only familiarity with Paris came from reading Hemingway's, A Movable Feast and all the Maigret mysteries he could lay his hands on.

I'm not sure of his original plan while in Paris but I do know how he passed the time. His day started at a small café on a corner of the rue Dragon in the Latin Quarter. He ordered the same morning repast every day _ coffee and a croissant. There is enough similarity between coffee and café to remove any confusion and croissant is now as much a part of the English vocabulary as the French. He passed the morning with the Herald Tribune which if you read every word and finish all the puzzles can fill the entire morning. His good fortune is the French custom of leaving you alone at your table until you make the decision to get up and leave. Most afternoons were filled with English language movies and evenings, eyes glued to CNN. Now that CNN is world wide it has become the saviour of many homesick sabbaticants.

The problem of what to eat and where was soon overcome

when he discovered the wide availability of McDonalds in the culinary capital of the world. He worked his way through each and every McDonalds in Paris and sampled every item on the menu. Being a methodical individual he developed a comparative rating scheme on each item for each outlet to help decide who should be honoured with his repeat business. Upon completion he sent a copy to the McDonalds headquarters as a thank you for providing nourishment to body and intellect during his exile in Paris. McDonalds responded by hiring him to direct their store evaluations worldwide. He is now a very rich former academic.

The most famous of the sabbatical applicants at my own institution of renown was the economist who applied for and received funding to conduct a survey of the world's major ports. He returned with a marvelous slide show of New York, London, Geneva, Hong Kong, Shanghai, Beijing, Sydney, Buenos Aires, Rio de Janeiro, Mexico City, Denver and San Francisco. A remarkable thing about the show is there wasn't a single port picture. And I'm not sure all of the places really are ports. I did notice some very attractive skiing shots from Switzerland and Colorado.

The application not only serves as justification for granting the sabbatical but a record to compare with what you did. Now that is a scary possibility, someone knocking on your office door upon your return, application in hand a leer splitting their lips and the words, "Welcome back, now let's sit down and have a chat about how you made out on your sabbatical." In other words, "Explain why you didn't do what you said you would do." Not too worry because although grist for the mill of nightmares that is all it is. A fear that exists only in your dreams. I have never seen, or heard of anyone doing an audit on sabbatical activities. To borrow from a good old boys saying, "What happens on the sabbatical road stays on the sabbatical road." Sort of reminiscent of the days in government before some short sighted fool screwed it all up by hiring an Auditor-General who took the job seriously. So far we in the Crypt have avoided that mistake.

Now 99% of the people who become eligible for a sabbatical get it. The 1% exception is my faculty club drinking buddy Harv. As in so many things Harv's problem is excess. One of his favorite drinking phrases about the time the letter S turns into a prolonged hiss is, "If it's worth doing, it's worth doing to excess." At his last sabbatical he not only didn't do the research project he put in his application, he didn't do any research and he didn't show up at the university where the Dean had pulled strings to achieve his acceptance, with private office no less. The problem came to light at Harv's annual review. Since he had done nothing else that year all that was left for discussion was, "What did you do on your sabbatical?" Harv's response was he thought he could make more of a contribution working on a theoretical problem in the solitude of his home surroundings. The next time Harv applied for a sabbatical the Dean's memory took on pachyderm proportions.

As for myself, I've conservatively stuck to the location of the application, even though the activities bear unfamiliar resemblance to my plans. If I had the perspicacity and foresight of the McDonalds analyst in Paris I might have turned my times in Edinburgh and Paris into a resounding success. If I had only kept notes and developed a rating scheme for the pubs and wine bars of my experience who knows what riches I may now roll in.

As I now see the end of my sentence inside the Crypt I have but one sabbatical left and must make it memorable.

At one time my thoughts and pleasures turned more to the exotica of the cosmopolitan. London and Paris were never far from my top choices. Now as the remaining hair lightens and the bones age, fantasies of the warm and exotic hang at the forefront. So I guess it would be no surprise when I bring up the Caribbean and Hawaii as leading contenders. I don't know whether to flip a coin and pick one or go all out and do both. Hey, maybe I could contact the McDonalds guy and develop a comparative rating scale to help people make such decisions.

Episode

What's It All About

BUCKS OR BRAINS? Which does the university stand for? Too simple? OK, I plead mea culpa. But at times the debate doesn't seem to stray far from that simple dichotomy.

A short moment of reflection will stretch the list of patrons who have a more than passing interest in the life and lessons of the university. Non – academic staff who look to the university for income and one day a secure pension. Employers in need of trained and educated workers and training programs to retread those whose best before date has long since passed. Parents who want their off-spring educated or at least certified enough to obtain employment beyond burger flipping. Alumni who want to be remembered and hope the reputation of their alma mater grows to further enhance their certification, no matter what they remember from the classroom. The community who basks in the reflected glory of their learned institution and often find it a source of solace and entertainment in sports and the arts. Research granting agencies, public and private, who seek to demonstrate that without their largesse the world would be more impoverished than it is.

All of the above have a legitimate claim to the goings on in the Crypt but to include Uncle Tom Cobbley and all in this slim tome is too much. As in all of life limits exist and choices must be made. The choice for now is the one that preoccupied the portion of the waking hours that I gave to the inhabitants of the university _ faculty and students. Now within the faculty group are various divisions and where there is division it follows as a hound on a bitch in heat that conflict in all its various and curious forms will burst forth. A further distinction that will become important as we proceed is disciplinary background. It can produce wars that make those based in religion look like a minor school ground fracas.

Within the student tribe there are many sub tribes of significance such as arts, science, professional and a further distinction may be found in number of years a student has been interred within the Crypt, which includes that particular brand of inmate who tries to look like faculty since they usually harbour such aspirations but end up acting like students. I of course speak of graduate students.

It has been said that the educational ideal is best exemplified in the quiet shadows of a wooded glen with the teacher on one end of a mossy log and the student on the other joined in a search for wisdom and truth. Harvey says bull fluff, more progress would be made if the teacher sat on the student and talked to the log. Now I wouldn't want to say that is a widely held belief among the denizens of the Crypt but neither is it totally beyond the experience of those who reside therein.

The faculty presumably take up the calling because of a deep and abiding interest in their subject of study. It is something they care about to the point of obsession. In the extreme all else is put aside in exchange for time devoted to their research. In a slightly different context George Bernard Shaw caught the idealistic stereotype in his reference to an artist.

> "The true artist will let his wife starve, his children go barefoot, his mother drudge for his living at seventy, sooner than work at anything but his art."
>
> *Major Barbara*

Substitute academic for artist and you have the idealistic stereotype of the academic scholar. Of course this is a stereotype but like all good stereotypes it contains at least a kernel of truth. For true academics research is central to their work and life. At least it is at one point in their career even if their obsession lacks legs that carry them to retirement. After all, a PhD must be earned based upon some sort of research.

Since research is of great importance to the academic tribe great energy is expended to place and keep it at the centre of the university galaxy. The stars that shine brightest in the academic galaxy are those who learn to pick the plumpest of cherries. Their research leads the field and the major granting agencies seek them out to spend their largesse. They are the ones who pocket the international prizes that bear the name Nobel or similar and carry them home to decorate their trophy shelf along with cheques to fatten the bank account.

While the stars are well rewarded their influence and contribution extends beyond their own personal space.

Students, in theory, have the opportunity to learn from the world's scientific leaders. That is if the stars find their way into the classroom. And here IF is spelled in capitals because the reward for research is time for more research and everyone knows where the time is found. But the stars of science enhance the reputation of the institution and therefore spill over onto anyone who has ever attended as a student so all is not lost. Sort of like the old English expression, 'My father knew Lord George.'

Since research output is a universal product that easily crosses borders the community at large does stand to benefit. Sort of an early form of globalization. Once upon a time the research was made freely available to all comers. In recent times the powers in charge have recognized the pecuniary aspects of research. It can lead to saleable products. Rare indeed is the university without an office to turn research into cash and a phalanx of support personnel to help with marketing and interpret the dark meaning of intellectual property law. Now the commercial offices of biological and information technology are located within an easy commute of the great learning centres of the world.

No matter the advances on the research and commercial front, there are many who think the prime raison d'être is the continued education and socialization of our youth. Students occupy frontal position in this interest parade with the unanimous support of their parents and general public, when they think about it. It is fortunate for the students and the university at large that while important, the number of true stars in the academic firmament is few. The vast majority of we academic toilers occupy a middling position where our research contribution is at the fringe of the discipline. Its not that we don't yearn for centre stage but, numero uno is a crowded position. It is among our middling group that you find the mass of teaching talent. For some this is a good thing because they find teaching to be pleasurable and rewarding. It is in the same group that teaching finds their champions who argue for more resources devoted to instruction and greater recognition at the crucial career junctures of promotion and tenure. For others, well, as in Harv's case there is always the faculty club.

But what does one enter on the blank computer screen under Class Objectives and Course Outline. Those of us who do the filling out have it bred in the bone, or at least pounded into the head bone during the brain washing experience of graduate school that we owe fealty to the discipline. Whether they like it or not those who appear before us in the classroom will hear and supposedly benefit from the deep knowledge of our discipline, whatever it may be. What happens beyond the classroom in terms of personal or practical application is not our concern. We are there to teach the yearning students what we know and for reasons beyond our knowledge they have chosen to sit at our feet and soak it up.

Not only will they learn a particular subject matter but also general skills to serve throughout a lifetime of toil and personal renewal. Here I speak of such generalizable skills beyond the bounds of any discipline, such as learning how to learn, problem solving and development of communication in all oral and written forms, although the latter is now usually translated as Power Point.

Now all of this is well and good for those of us anchored by soul and employment within the Crypt of Academe. It is less the case for those assembled at the annual convocation who hope that when they sortie forth into the outside world that the magic in the wave of their diploma will conjure up employment opportunities of challenge and financial reward. Not to put too fine on a point on it but the issue I speak of is will their four years of toil and financial penury end in a JOB. If not they may think they should have become a plumber like Uncle Elmer, or increasingly Aunt Ethel.

It is not only the students who express deep concern on the employment issue but so too the payers of the piper. Less and less is Professor Piper calling the tune in the world of academe and some would say about time too. The paying parents who pony up some of the cash, the governments who pony up more and an increasingly indebted student body are shouting out their favorite academic jingles that they expect to be played and sung with gusto.

A further expression of the issue is found in the allocation of funds within the university. It is not surprising that the grandest buildings and most well endowed chairs are found in the sciences, engineering and the professions. It is usually presumed this is merely their just reward for being up close to the job market and the continued economic progress of the planet. And of course more recently the saviours of the planet from environmental obliteration. It appears that our wee piece of terra firma is trilling the words of Bob Dylan and we truly are on the road to destruction. That is outside of a few solitary and rarely heard voices of dissent.

The liberal arts counter that it is unfair and unwise to neglect their central place inside the Crypt. They are more and more resorting to an economic argument that their graduates are highly employable in the job market and may in the long term surpass other graduates in the economic return from their years of study. I must say it does surprise me of late when I read that the background of a female entrepreneur includes a firm grounding in philosophy with a master's thesis on Schopenhauer and yesterday the business channel featured a woman with an Honours degree in English who leads one of the more successful mutual funds. With the amassing of such powerful data the arts community is upping the ante on the amounts and decibel levels for improved funding.

The arguments are brought into the academic wars over curriculum and the need for at a least a modicum of liberal background for all graduates if they are to be considered educated beyond the level of cave dwellers. This argument at times falls on deaf ears among students of the engineering and the scientific community who see time spent on such arcane subjects as Sociology and English as time away from their true vocation and a negative effect come job time. The less polite say it is only a make work project to justify employment for already over bloated departments in the Arts. The reply is for such philistines to remove themselves and set up a technical university as found in Europe and sometimes the USA and thereby leave the true nature of the university pure and unsullied by avarice and worldly thoughts.

Such arguments have waged for eons and will for further eons. If they didn't gatherings around committee tables in the august halls of the administration at money sharing time – i.e. budgets and the beer tables of the faculty club would result in attendance nearing zero.

But making light of such issues should not detract from their importance. Education has often been seen as the great leveler. The one place where even those of an unfortunate background may, with talent, skill and hard work rise above the busted flush that society dealt them at birth.

Society and those of us in it will be the worse off for having failed at the task. Never should we give up the debate _ brains or bucks.

15

Episode

Up, Up and Away

THE MEASURE OF a student? What should it be? And who decides? Once upon a time it was the personage at the front of the classroom, usually called professor. Now it's more of a negotiated arrangement involving those in the seats. With those same seat holders often dictating terms. I know from today's painful experience. Curt came back, like he'd never been away.

I was sitting at my desk, an uncommon event, struggling over an innovation in statistical analysis described in one of the journals I receive as part of a professional membership. I skim it on occasion to see what my grad school mates are up to, but today the article consumed my full attention. The authors had said unkind things about one of my former contributions. I had long since consigned that bit of doggerel to the memory dump. However, for some reason the authors had invaded the archives and dug it up like common grave robbers.

I wanted to put them in their place with a scathing rejoinder. I searched their scribblings for errors of logic, fact or anything and found none. I had one alternative left, attack the research methodology and statistical analysis. I really must keep up on such things in the future, no matter the boredom quotient. My deflated ego suffered another blow when a sinister presence chilled the room.

I knew who before I saw his face. As I raised my eyes from the sinful article I recognized the shapeless baggy pants. A curling sneer confirmed the sighting. "Hello Curt, I didn't hear your knock."

"You wouldn't if I didn't."

When a pillar of your support structure falters there is a perverse comfort in the stability of any aspect of your life. Even if the name is Curt.

Students only show up in my office for a solitary reason and passing the time of day or going out for a beer is never on the list. Grades are now the primary reason for visitations. I do remember in times of long ago debates over matters of academic interest and import, or even recent newspaper headlines on topics other than sport.

I decided that Curt had no intention of going away so we might as well proceed to the pain at hand. I offered him the only chair in the room not filled with books or articles of clothing. He declined and said he didn't expect to be here that long. I think he preferred to stand in front of and therefore over me. I'm sure he thought it a major advantage in the about to begin verbal joust. At least I hoped nothing beyond verbal.

He didn't wait for me to raise any questions about his presence or even enquire after his health or those near and dear to him. Neither did he feel any need to make such solicitous enquiries of myself. Not wanting to give up too much at the start I merely asked the reason for his presence.

"The B⁺ you gave me in that crap class of yours."

I choose to ignore the negative descriptor of my class since I knew that Curt's linguistic capability allowed for a more graphic and scatological description. Instead I opted for my preferred defense mechanism, the open question gambit.

"Tell me why you think a B⁺ is not the appropriate grade for your work in class.?" I could have said for work not in class since he rarely attended but I didn't want to raise the stakes too early in our exchange.

And he did. I'm sorry I didn't have a tape recorder. Or even better a camcorder. But I didn't, so must rely on the written word to relay my best recollection of events. He launched into why he could not tolerate anything less than an 'A' on his record. And the reason for such an exalted record is to ensure entry into the best of law schools. He didn't stop there but continued that he had lived in penury long enough and saw the practice of law as the way out. What's more he knew a lot of lawyers became politicians so in case he wanted to enter politics and continue up the ladder to Prime Minister he thought it good preparation. It crossed my mind that maybe I should lower his grade to save us from placing him in any position of power that might threaten our lives or livelihood.

I tried again, asking Curt if he could explain where and how my acute myopia had missed identifying the genius of his work. Curt found any line of enquiry that relied on logic and a carefully honed argument as irrelevant and switched to the fairness counter. He pointed out that the absurd (his word) Tweedle duo had both received at least an A⁻. He considered it only fair that a regular guy like himself should do at least as well and to be truly fair, better, therefore an A.

I shuffled through the mélange of papers et al that covered my desk, not to find anything, but as a delaying tactic to collect my thoughts. At the instant I dropped my lower jaw to reply, the Tweedles pirouetted into the room. They trilled in an appropriate exchange:

> You like tomato and I like tomahto;
> Potato, potahto, tomato, tomahto!
> Let's call the whole thing off!

"See," Curt yelped!

I granted, to myself, that he had a point.

This time the Tweedles presented in monochrome outfits. The dazzling Dee in what I might describe as magenta, truly a grape ripe for the picking. The daring Dum, a.k.a Don, had been attracted to a chartreuse ensemble. No doubt the vine that supported Dee. To round off the outfits Dee had pointed shoes and an Andy Capp flat cap of the same colour as her brother's outfit, and for Dum, vice versa. There was no mistaking them, nor would they get lost in a crowd of any size.

Curt faded into the shadows of the background overwhelmed by the dazzle of the Tweedle's presence. They quickly announced the reason for their arrival - to tell me face-to-face how much they liked my class.

I immediately lost control of my vocal chords, but not my eyesight. I couldn't miss a glower from Curt.

The Tweedles launched into a falsetto duet of a verse from AABA's, 'Thank You for the Music':

> So I say thank you for the music
> For giving it to me
> So I say thank you for the music

For giving it to me.

I beamed and said it was a pleasure and they were a pair of 'Super Troupers.' Curt bent over and jammed his fore finger so far down his throat I thought he'd gag for real.

At that moment the Tweedles spied Curt in the corner. They exchanged introductions according to their roles_ the Tweedles beaming, Curt glowering. I pointed out that Curt was here for the same reason as the Tweedles _ grades. But of a different nature. He was unhappy. The Tweedles happy.

In an instant Curt had two allies for his cause. Dee and Dum said they never liked to see someone unhappy and why not give Curt the same grade they had received?

"Why not give everyone the same grade, who needs distinctions," I replied.

I could see that Curt did not like the idea because without distinctions how could there be a list of betterers and worsers for law school. What criteria then _ darts? I knew the Tweedles of the world wouldn't mind but not the Curts. But the Curts only care if they are top of the heap.

For amusement and because I do have a perverse side to my nature I asked how the Tweedles would like it if I accepted their argument but lowered their grade to a B+, the same as Curt. That wiped the grin off their face for a nanosecond but wanting to be consistent with their position they agreed. Curt did not.

I glanced at my watch and panicked. I gave it a shake but no movement. It displayed the correct time. By now Harv would be well into his second jug at the faculty club. I expressed my regrets but claimed a need to rush off and give blood to a grievously ill great aunt. In parting I confirmed there would be no change to the Tweedles grade but

I would take another look at Curt's record for the term. As I rushed past them I said they could close the door behind them. Curt gave me the first smile of his life. Well more along the lines of a self satisfied smirk that said couldn't you have done this at the start and not wasted my time. Once again the squeaky worm gets the grease.

I arrived at the faculty club red faced and puffing. I explained my lateness in terms of being accosted by students to jack up their grades. Harv harrumphed in sympathy. He said it's a problem of epidemic proportions. Beyond anything going on in the economy and worse than all predictions of a pandemic.

More as devil's advocate than a believer I said, "Some people think it's the result of improved teaching and better students."

"Bull feathers," he said. "I don't see change in the badly dressed and disinterested wretches who drone on at the front of the classroom. Nor do I believe in any significant advance in the gene pool of the sleepy crowd on the opposite side."

He blamed it on the high schools raising grades beyond realistic levels to help their graduates sneak into institutions of higher learning beyond their native capability. Of course it's a strategy easily copied and now everyone's doing it. Then upon arrival on our doorstep very few have experienced the icy awakening of anything less than a B and now more and more nothing less than an A. Aided by rampant student power and the threat of student ratings along with video supported blogs most of my colleagues opt for, 'Anything for a go along to get along strategy.' I think that's what someone said about Richard Nixon's entourage during the suppression of the Watergate tapes.

Where will it end? I'm not sure but I do recall a story the economists like to tell about the Great Inflation of the Roman Empire that goes more or less as follows. A series of emperors substituted more and more of the silver in their currency, the denarius, with copper or bronze. As a result prices went up, up and away. Rather than taking responsibility for the debasement of the currency the emperor blamed it on the greed of his subjects and threatened death for price increases. All to no avail. It took a century to settle the problem when a new gold coin, the bezant, became the currency.

What does this have to do with soaring grades? Maybe nothing.

16

Episode

Who Rules?

"ARTERIOSCLEROSIS, THAT'S THE answer," Harv muttered into his beer and wrote it down on a pad he pulled out of his plaid shirt pocket. I noticed he had been using a good portion of the pad for a game of X and Os. As far as I could tell he lost most of the time.

I knew he hadn't detected my stealth like arrival so as he raised a full glass of suds to his lips I cupped my hand under my armpit and made a loud farting noise. Immature, boyish prank more suited to an IQ challenged Peter Pan than a graying professorial member of the Crypt? No doubt, but Harv's gasp and drenching of his beer belly had the desired effect. I roared and he growled words that caused my mother to wash out my mouth with soap.

I apologized for the drenching of his pants and noted it might take some time for them to dry to the point where he could stand without aspersions cast on his urinary control. He said the mini brains of the world can keep their opinions to themselves, I really should apologize for the irrecoverable loss of his beer. In the interest of friendship I did and poured some of my jug into Harv's to replenish his loss of the golden liquid.

He yelped in protest that my domestic suds didn't match the quality of his imported selection. Hard to satisfy some people.

I asked him if some medic had been scoping out his arteries. He said not, rather he had been ruminating on his new game creation. He pointed out that often quackery clinicians or leaders of so-called motivational groups will ask the unsuspecting to describe themselves or significant other in terms of something of little direct relevance like an animal, fruit, flower or whatever. Harv thought it of more relevance and interest to look to a disease as a descriptor.

I feared the answer but asked the question anyway, "So who, from this time hence will become known as Arteriosclerosis?" Sounded like some Greek might fit.

"Not who, but what, the university of course," Harv replied. He thought arteriosclerosis fit perfectly _ 'a chronic disease characterized by abnormal thickening and hardening of the arterial walls with a resulting loss of elasticity'.

I had no rebuttal.

Harv's rumour mill had picked up the message that our president, who had always been a totally committed disciple of a policy of inertia had found a larger pond to float in. Our president always claimed her calm is the only way to manage the varying herds of cats roaming the halls of the Crypt. She enjoyed using the parable of the duck to describe her approach _ calm repose above the surface, swimming flat out below. Harv claimed more like catatonic, all the way down.

Episode 16 | Who Rules?

I had never been a member of the president's fan club, or anyone in an administrative position. I considered it one of my god given academic rights, along with tenure and freedom of speech, to hold administrators in complete and total disdain. Such is the nature of the Crypt. It is so written. At the same time they somehow seem to be a necessity. Kind of like the inevitable end result of a great gourmet dinner. Not necessarily pleasant but something that must and will happen.

To enliven our sudsy exchanges I decided to challenge Harv on his view of the president and all administrators, OK, goad would be closer to the mark. Unlike Harv's new disease based game this is an ancient and much practiced form of amusement among academicians. Harv is a practitioner of long experience and always a willing participant.

I moved first and proposed the brilliance of a policy of inertia. In a system where everyone is convinced they come first and take orders from no one it is the only realistic alternative. Anyone who can sit patiently until all around exhaust their arguments and expend all their interest and resources is bound to triumph at the end of the day. Or put simply, let them shoot their load and roll on. I continued that our soon to depart president had learned her lesson well from the grim and unforgiving graduate school of experience.

Harv pointed out that it shouldn't have been that way. The president had moved into the palatial office suite, bathroom and shower included, sporting an academic record of sufficient renown that great things were and should have been expected.

No doubt I replied but what did that have to do with running the university. Another case of someone being hired with a great background in an area that has nothing to do

105

with their new job. I'm sure the denizens of many another Crypt can relate the same story.

The new incumbent rushes in full of wonderful ideas to make drastic changes and raise the sites of all inhabitants to search for and find new stars. To fight the impossible dream and become more than we thought we could be. Tad bit of hyperbole? Of course but one has to do something to raise the blood. Unfortunately, the hackles may rise along with the blood.

Well, she could have been a little more diplomatic in dealing with the deans of all the departments was Harv's rejoinder. Trying to tell them that if any department under their guidance wasn't in at least the top two in the country, or third with a chance to move up, was in serious jeopardy of joining the black rhino on the most endangered species list. The only way to account for such out of character behaviour by any well schooled academic is someone must have passed on one of those books put out by a former corporate CEO trying to burn his name into posterity by sharing ancient corporate wisdom and war stories. And picking up a healthy advance along the way.

I replied that it caught their attention enough to pass it on to department chairs who used it to try and scare the members of the department. I remember it being a topic of discussion at all of two department meetings. Most items from department meetings disappear immediately or become lost in some committee review. Well of course that ended it, didn't it? The message was sent down the line until it was ground into dust under the feet of the shuffling foot soldiers in the professorial ranks. Life goes on, as usual.

Harv allowed that I did have a point. The only time he remembered any serious change about to take place was when the president did think a case could be made to eliminate an unmentioned faculty. The argument was substandard research, not on the radar of anyone in the field and anything they professed to do was readily available at other nearby institutions where it was done better. All the cash raised from the trimming could be reallocated to more deserving departments who would move us further into the ranks of the great and good, thereby attracting accomplished students and most important, major cash infusions.

The presidential office thought they had a slam dunk on this one. The president assembled a team who thought like herself led by two vice-presidents of impeccable credentials. They thought a clear rational argument buttressed by the best of hard data and the more the better would carry the day. Fools!

To make the change the case had to be presented to and passed by the university senate. An august body of all the interest groups on campus including academics, students and administrative staff or as some would say, Uncle Tom Cobbley and All. Now it's clear to anyone that you don't convince a group of such varied and dispersed interests with charts and numbers. You do it by getting the interest groups on side and that means an appeal to the guts, not the knot atop the shoulders. The threatened departments gathered an amazing range of tearful testimonials how they had changed the lives of so many while under the tutelage of the great, but now maligned members of the threatened departments. The result _ no contest. The departments remain and have expanded more than the tribe of Abu Ben Adhem.

Harv slouched further into his chair, frowned and to my

surprise admitted that maybe I'm right. In a system where the status quo is the norm, best act accordingly until the opposition is looking the other way and jump at the chance.

But then Harv hit me with a real conundrum. "So does it make any difference who is in charge? Like whom do you think would do the best job, the current incumbent, you, me or Bambi?"

I allowed that he and I were automatically excluded because we'd never show up at the interminable meetings. And that was a must for all administrators, presidents included. That left Bambi and the incumbent.

In an uncharacteristic stroke of genius Harv hit upon the answer. "Image is everything, Bambi for President."

And we'd campaign under the presidential slogan of Warren G. Harding.

"Return to normalcy."

17

Episode

Every Year

WE DO IT every year. The Annual Meeting. No doubt why we call it the Annual Meeting. For Crypt dwellers it's the biggest, funnest gig of the year. A time when academic professionals travel from all corners of the world to celebrate us.

Each and every professional group in the Crypt has one. The words of exchange vary in keeping with the secret rituals of the professions but in the grand scheme of things they're all from the same cookie cutter. Of course we scamper around the country to other gatherings to show our face and wave the flag but none match the importance and grandeur of the Annual Meeting.

The highlight for me is a long, boozy reunion dinner with my former grad school mates. We call ourselves the Three Stooges, plus Greta. I'm Curly. Shep and Moe played football in high school days but on opposing teams. The rivalry continues but in true academic spirit at a verbal level. Greta always marched to her own drum but loved to share company over booze and food. I wanted to opt for the Three Musketeers and Greta could be D'Artignan but could never make the case. Some kind of Francophobia by my mates.

We transited from boozing buddies to the tightest of groups the night we broke into the department chair's office. Greta made us do it. She was afraid she had failed her comps and couldn't stand the suspense of waiting for the official results. So she talked, conned, brow beat the three of us into becoming accomplices.

It happened on the way home after a boozy night. As we passed campus Greta flashed the news that we were about to cross the line into the realm of B&E artists. I'm not sure if it was alcoholic courage that sealed our fate or the prospects of Greta in our debt.

When we arrived at the door to the chair's office Shep asked the obvious question that no one seemed to have thought of up to that point. How do we get in? No problem for Greta, out came a pin and in a flash we were through the door. I volunteered for look-out duty while the others searched the inner sanctum. Security was much more lax in days of yore. They found the exams in record time. Greta had passed with high honours. A note had been included from one of the examiners that said, "A rare find, body after Marilyn Monroe, brain after Einstein." Greta made a copy and has it in a frame that hangs in her bathroom.

I know all three of us tried to call in the marker from Greta and we all received the same answer. "I can get laid any time but true friends are hard to come by. Thanks but no thanks." Until we shared the story on graduation day I'm sure each of us thought he was the only one that had been shut out.

I know being in a group with only 25% female representation is below the politically correct norm but that's about what it is for now throughout most Crypts. But change is in the offing, since student enrollment of the female gender passed 50% a few years ago in nearly all faculties. Justice is served claims Greta.

As always I arrived first to down a thirst quenching beer. Martinis make a poor thirst quencher. I know from ample experience. I positioned myself to be ready as official greeter. Greta stepped into the room as the last sip slid down my throat. I had no sooner finished a hug and lightning two cheek continental kiss than Shep and Moe cut in to finish the ritual. Next move, a round of celebratory cocktails.

Martinis all round on the male side of the table. To avoid sipping from the wrong glass I marked mine with a single olive, Shep a twist and Moe an onion. Greta always searches the menu for something exotic in bright colours and lots of fruit. The drinks at last in hand we raised our glasses to the traditional Scottish toast: "Wae's like us? Damn few and they's a deid."

The official raison d'être of the Annual Meeting is a cel-ebration of academic achievements by swapping tales of recent scholarly pursuits with like-minded souls. The tale swapping takes place in small cells lacking windows and barely enough air to sustain life. Moe had just escaped from said event, his ego much in need of a martini. A quick first called for a second.

An almost forgotten research project had turned up a set of counter intuitive results. A rare event in any scholar's life, no matter the area of pursuit. Being of a generous nature Moe wanted to share the results with his significant others. To say little of basking in a modicum of glory.

He pulled strings through Greta to appear last on the program for the final say and hope his words would be remembered well beyond everyone racing to the bar. A serious lapse of judgment. One of the earlier presenters rambled on in excess of her allotted time. Even when the chair requested she shorten her presentation the meager response was to talk faster.

"Bored beyond belief," said Moe, over the crunching of his onion. "She emptied the room, except for my present and former graduate students. And by the way, where were you lot?"

No glory for Moe. We supplicated and demanded he send us a copy of his work.

Shep did admit to a day of absence taking in the delights of the city. To show his eclectic bent he had spent a morning at the local art museum among a special exhibition of Egyptian artifacts. "Mummies and that sort of thing," he said. For a change of pace he had stumbled on a local watering hole famous for more imported draft beer on tap than anywhere on the planet.

"What, no strip joints," Greta asked?

"Tomorrow night," Shep replied. "Want to come?"

Greta returned a look that would make a penguin shiver.

"I'm in," I voted in a show of solidarity. I didn't admit to a secret hope that I might rediscover Daphne. The luster she gave my class and her talent on stage still warms my memory.

Now on his third martini Moe raised his glass and slurred, "Me too."

"Boys," snapped Greta.

Greta gently nursed her crimson cocktail and fished out the bits of fruit that had settled to the bottom. She usually awaits the end of the meal to catch up on the booze consumption and knock back a Napoleon class cognac. At one time she joined us in a cigar with the cognac but no longer. Of course now the anti-smoking storm troopers have conquered the restaurant world none of us do. Even if they had been defeated it wouldn't be considered proper for someone of her standing in the profession.

No one expected it of her in grad school days. Now she has moved to the forefront of the profession and is our Past President. Moe and Shep were marked as the ones most likely to succeed but somehow stumbled out of the gate. They both found first jobs in the most prestigious of Crypts and we lesser folk expected it would be all downhill after that. Not to be. Rather than face possible negative tenure decisions they moved on and down a rung or two on the ladder. We are all comfortably settled into a Crypt that matches our energy level, if not once held aspirations but enjoy basking in Greta's reflected glory and pronounce at every opportunity, "We were at grad school together."

Earlier in the day I noticed Greta working the hallways and coffee shops for some personal political purpose. Greta's a past master. Her ideas of where our profession should be headed and the role women must play lack ambiguity. She never misses a chance to lobby for support.

But at this meeting I noticed her huddled with special representatives from unarguably the most prestigious Crypt of our profession. I thought it was time for me to take centre stage at the table. Lacking subtly I blurted out, "Greta our dear, are you planning a change of location or just fishing for an offer to gain negotiating leverage at the home Crypt."

Ever coy she admitted to mutual interest but had not

made up her mind.

That meant in no uncertain terms she was moving into a prestigious research chair if the numbers were right. And what better place for the announcement than the Annual Meeting.

"Will you still talk to us," asked Moe?

"And dine with us each year," came from Shep?

"Of course," said Greta. "After that grind at good old Grad U we're joined forever. Call it academic polygamy."

"Anyone who could survive the grind of comps and a thesis together must stick together," Moe replied. "And committed a felony together," Shep said.

I took advantage of a moment of silence whilst my dearly beloveds took a sip and jumped in, "How could we miss the Annual Meeting? Where and when else do we have an opportunity to visit exotic parts of the world, share the company of some of the most important people in our lives and all in the name of professional obligation on an expense account."

"Some of us still make professional contributions," Greta said with a bit of an edge to her voice. Always the conscience of the group, dear Greta. A year never passes that she isn't a major participant. Who could do without her?

Or the Annual Meeting.

18

Episode

Measuring Up. Or Down?

MEASURE! WE DO it all the time. Little could be more central to the Crypt.

We measure students. We measure our brethren at life altering moments of tenure and promotion. We measure our fellow Crypt dwellers at sister institutions in games of invidious comparison. Some of us even measure our fellow citizens. The powerful and influential being the usual targets of attention. What's more fun than pouring boiling verbal oil from the parapets onto the great and good, be they socialites, people of affairs (in a business sense of course) or poncey politicos.

I'm sure it's obvious who orchestrates it all. Us! We hold the yardstick. Hell, we even design and craft the yardstick and make up the rules of application. Such is the natural order and how the world should turn so long as God remains in her heavens and looks down with benevolence, or at least benign neglect.

117

The exams students write are of our making and we decide the grades. The criteria for tenure and promotion are of our making and we do the judging. And when the external world comes under scrutiny we choose the target and fire the verbal ammunition.

But the cosmos has taken on a new order. Now the object of measurement is Us. I don't mean the classroom rating game that I commented on at length in a previous episode. At least in that game the players are still Crypt insiders. No, I mean the ratings game designed to boost sales of the nation's leading publications. A measurement game conducted by outsiders.

I had a slim awareness of the activity but had managed to navigate most days without intrusion into my core life. Harv changed all that today when we convened at the faculty club.

Since my arm fart trick he has taken to positioning himself with his back to the wall. No more sneak attacks on Harv. He of little faith and less trust. He spied my entry from behind a recent popular publication read by the masses, but rarely citizens of the Crypt.

"We're down this year," Harv proclaimed and drained his pint to half mast.

"What's down, beside the contents of your beer glass?"

He set the paper on the table, turned toward me and made a red circle with his favorite marking pen. The table had a this year, last year comparison and this year's ranking counted one less than last year.

I'm actually less concerned about the actual rank of our revered institution than where we are relative to the homes of my significant others. I noticed we were further up the table than where Shep and Mo hang their mortar boards.

A just verdict. I also noted that we lag the home of dear Greta, a natural expectation. I also saw that my Ph D alma mater maintained a position near the top which reflected the credibility of my pedigree. A thankful result.

I related all this to Harv, who shot back a stinging rebuke.

"Let shame cover you in stinking filth. You should leap to the ramparts and demand our return to glory. If we're not careful there could be more to this than ego. What about a loss of top students, a less favorable result at budget time from the government and granting agencies. To say little of disgruntled alumni with locked cheque books. It could body slam your Quality of Life."

Bit over the top I thought but that's Harv. In an attempt at a return to reason I mused, "So what do we have to up, what gets measured?" And took out my own favorite red marking pen and wrote down Harv's recitation.

A cursory glance at my list revealed a hodge podge of anything you might put a ruler to that's readily available in and about a Crypt. Such things as size of library, i.e. number of books, faculty credentials (publication, grants won and Ph Ds completed) and demographic mix, a number of items about students, like grades from high school, rate of graduation and services available to students and of course the financial circumstances of the institution, including scholarships.

A curiously mixed bag I thought and asked what kind of grinder sliced and diced everything and then boiled and bubbled it into a single brew that magically produced a rank order from top to bottom of our universities. Harv said no one but the raters knew, and maybe not them.

"Oh," I murmured.

Not only are the items measured apples and alligators, some carry a bigger bite than others. When queried on the subject Harv agreed and apparently so do the raters. Some criteria carry a heavier burden than their lesser brethren. But the allocation of weights is lost in the internal mists of the secret computer program that burps out the results.

A further complication to my jaundiced eye is comparability of so many items from one institution to the next. I guess a book is a book no matter the library where you do the counting. But it is common knowledge that high school grades are manipulated in many places to assist the less gifted graduates attain entry above their intellectual station. Some universities have turned to making adjustments to the grades of some high schools. In others a lively remedial learning process has been started to remove entrants from the ranks of illiterate and numerically challenged. I gather they are being staffed by faculty members who are not at the top of the research game. Something else that increases Harv's bar bill.

Harv allowed this to be the case and added that it had the same effect on our new president as sandpaper hidden in the toilet paper. The claim is we are unfortunate enough to live in and draw our students from high schools that have resisted the temptation to manipulate graduation grades. The average grades of our tender freshman (freshperson?) class are blow the national average and so down the table we go.

I also noted that all the measures might be classified as input variables. Things that go into the educational process that is supposed to transform an undergraduate from a raw and unschooled lump of clay into a learned and sophisticated individual who will improve her lot in life and in so doing that of all fellow citizens.

While Harv absented himself from my presence to attend to the inevitable result of drinking beer I ruminated on our dilemma. Harv has developed the unique skill of reaching for his beer glass as he lowers himself into his chair in one smooth movement so that by the time his butt hits the chair the glass is at his lips. At that same moment a simple question came to mind.

"Harv, never mind any other issues, where and how do the raters lay hands on the data. Surely not a random numbers table?"

"Not sure about the random numbers table but a lot used to come from us," Harv replied.

"So somebody recognized the problem of self-report data and put an end to it?"

"Nope," Harv replied in the middle of a slurp. "Like students, a lot of universities didn't like the grade they received and refused to play the game."

"Now what?"

"They do it anyway with whatever they can turn up from government and public sources," was Harv's less than helpful reply.

We seemed to have hit an impasse that even more beer wouldn't help. But it did. As soon as I returned with a recharged mug I saw a smile on Harv's face. He had an answer and so did I. I said, "I know what to do."

And Harv said, "Me too."

"Cooperate," we shouted in unison. "That's right go back to providing key data and make sure the publications get the right data and also make sure they get the results right."

Now I was on a roll and hit on a second idea. What a day. Two ideas in one day. I told Harv to make it all legit there should be output measures to see if the students did learn more at some institutions than others. And who better to do the measuring than the experts on measuring student output. Us. We just had to make sure we controlled the process all the way from front to back.

It's so good to be back in charge.

19

Episode

Quietly Into the Sunset. Or Sunrise?

WHERE DO WE come from?

What are we?

Where are we going?

Funny how Paul Gauguin's most famous painting comes to mind as I survey my now bare office walls. I have to be gone by day's end so the new tenant can shuffle in her academic paraphernalia at first light tomorrow morning. A number of her boxes already line the hallway like anti-tank traps. I'm not sure if she's afraid that someone is going to jump her claim or she's just over anxious to start hanging pictures. If I was a gentleman I'd move some of them in right away. If? Instead I sit here disposing of the tag end of a bottle of sherry that had reposed forgotten at the back of a bottom desk drawer. A welcome surprise. I thought I'd have to await my rendezvous with Harv at the faculty club before I could raise a celebratory glass.

The view from my corner office follows the river bank into the city centre towers of concrete and glass that glint to a copper sheen at sunset. Beyond lies the velvet green of our city's most exclusive golf course. My little world fulfills all three of the major canons of prime real estate _ location, location, location.

Office allocation used to be a simple and rule bound matter based entirely on rank and seniority. The person with the most seniority in the highest rank had first crack when an office came free. Neither race, colour, creed or demographic deficiency entered into it, nor did number of publications or any form of award. That's how I got this office. One of our younger colleagues housed on a lower floor looking out upon the brick wall of the adjacent build- ing pointed out the inequity of the system. He argued that it rewarded the old lags past their best before date who should be relegated to the basement so their lengthen- ing shadows wouldn't shade the light of our shining young stars. A prime office should be an incentive for proper and productive behaviour.

The dean jumped on the idea, claimed all offices as his and allocation his sole right. One more bauble to dangle for invidious comparison and hidden jealousies. My office was thrown into a package to seal the deal to attract a young and rising star. I remember her effusive compliments during our interview as she looked dreamily out the window. Her questions of me were more about the view than the job. The main reason I voted against her. I think she found out since there was only one negative vote at decision time. No doubt why she so anxiously awaits my departure before claiming her territory.

I had never planned to leave my sinecure at an early

date. But that is not unusual since plan is a foreign word to me. Harv calls me a hip shooter. A contributing factor to a number of scars _ physical and emotional. My reply is Harv couldn't shoot from the hip because he's always sitting on it.

The Big Minds that look after the big thinking for our Crypt decided one day that we needed a renewal. There had not been enough natural turnover and at every convocation, award ceremony or Christmas party the same old faces came into view. In the corporate world this annoyance might have been dealt with by a surprise welcome from a security guard who showed you the door while the lock on your office was changed. Such a soft alternative is less available among the not quite wheelchair bound tenured members of the Crypt. If the blunt instrument of showing the door cannot be relied upon another alternative must be found. The Big Minds hit upon bribery. A financial incentive that polite circles refer to as a buy-out.

At first I didn't pay much attention to the idea until I started to flip through the pages of the offer at the faculty club awaiting Harv's arrival. One of the rare days I beat him to the beer. I started to do a back of the envelope calculation and soon came to the conclusion that I likely wouldn't live long enough to accumulate as much money as I would get in a single cheque if I agreed to clean out my office and make way for fresh blood. And I would also start getting a generous payment each month called a pension. In return for all the largesse I only had to agree to stay away.

A time comes for everything and I thought my time had now come to move on. To what I didn't know but hoped time might take care of that too. The spark of the classroom and a new research project no longer kicked up my heart rate. And my attendance at anything like a faculty meeting had descended to zero. Maybe the time had come for a personal rejuvenation.

When Harv finally settled in and swept the back of his hand across his moustache to clean off the foam I broached the question of him joining me. We arrived in the same year, might as well depart in the same year.

"Me, never," Harv growled. "I'd never make it so easy for them."

I asked several other colleagues. Most said they intended to decline the offer since they hadn't come up with an alternative way to fill the day. A few said they would if they could keep their office on the grounds of continued research. When I took a look at the group none had produced enough papers in recent years to stock a decent lavatory for more than a day. If rejuvenation is the game why keep the bodies around.

After I announced I would grab the money and run, word got around to various circles. Even the students.

Curt surprised me with his usual unannounced arrival at my door. Trepidation is the predominant feeling that courses through my nerves in his presence. Although this time he didn't flash his usual malicious sneer. Maybe he's becoming more subtle in his attack mode, or just sneakier.

I asked what I could do for him and he said nothing. He had come by to express his regrets at my departure since he had planned to take more courses with me. His comment left me slack jawed but relieved at no more Curt.

"Why," I croaked?

"You've always been the most challenging of my profs. At least you put up a fight before raising my grade and not always as much as I whined for. The others always give in as soon as they see me."

Since, like Mark Twain, I'll take any complement we shook hands and I wished him well in his prospective law career and said we should keep in touch. Who knows, I may need a pit bull lawyer one day and none could be more tenacious than Curt.

The Tweedles arrived the day I packed the few books I kept. I have no idea why I kept them since I hadn't opened any of them in ages. Probably an attempt at maintaining some link with my history. I gave away nearly all of my books to grad students on a first come, first served basis. It saved me the problem of packing and carting them away to I knew not where, and then what? Who needs a room full of out of date, mostly never read books?

The Tweedles, what a joyful site. At first their heads peering around the doorframe and then the bodies, arm-in-arm. They high stepped across the room, pirouetted in unison to end sitting on my desk facing me. By some magic Dee reached behind my right ear and pulled out a crepe rose and as I stared in amazement Dum produced a silver dollar that apparently had been wedged in my right nostril.

"Memories are made of this," they hummed. "We will miss you."

"Really," I replied in honest amazement.

"Oh yes, of all of our professors you recognized our creativity more than any. Even those in our own Fine Arts faculty."

They both came around my desk, gave me a hug and a kiss on the cheek. Hope none of the morality police saw the kiss. They danced backwards out the door and disappeared. I had detected a slight hint of cinnamon from Dee and peppermint from Dum. I may not wash my face for a day or two.

I sent an omnibus e-mail to Moe, Shep and Greta that my time to move on had come. I sometimes think Moe and Shep have a psychic joining at the hip. They both sent almost the same return e-mail. After duly chastising me for cowardice and leaving the field of battle much too early they finally condescended to congratulations and much jealousy at the mistake of joining an institution without the foresight to implement a similar plan.

The ever busy and popular Greta took almost a week to reply and mostly wrote about herself and why she could never retire early. Her argument had to do with all the important work she had underway or planned to start when she finished the current work. In other words she was too important to depart before her time and her time would never come.

Whatever scratching uncertainty I might have had about my decision disappeared when Bambi returned from a high school reunion. Although I think the scratching had more to do with a new soap I had been using than the decision. She pranced into my office with a glow on her face like a pussycat that had been awarded a lifetime supply of cream. She leaned over my desk so I was much too distracted to notice her hand until she covered her chest with it.

I reeled back in my chair so hard I think the wheels blackened the tile. I covered my eyes as though blinded by a bright light. She sported a diamond big enough to cover her finger up to the knuckle. An old flame had arrived at the high school without the encumbrance of a mate and they had an immediate and passionate reconnection. Bambi had agreed to change her marital status, her name and to help her new soul mate manage his house in Malibu, his apartment in Paris and his chalet on the slopes of St. Moritz.

Generous to the core, our beloved Bambi. I often said that when Bambi left I would follow her out the door.

Of course I had to sit through the obligatory good-bye lunch. The luncheon post mortem included the usual congratulations, bad jokes and false expressions of regret at my going and a few who said they wished their circumstances would let them abandon ship too. I wanted to say it only took a signature on the dotted line. The lunch ended with a handing over of gifts. My booty included a book on learning how to play golf, a painting of our building that every departee gets and leather bound copies of Joyce's, Ulysses and Proust's, In Search of Lost Time, along with a list of the remaining 100 greatest books of all time. I hadn't the heart to mention I had owned both books since my undergrad days. I bought them in the belief that one must read both books to be truly educated. I didn't get much past page 3 of either one and to this day remain truly uneducated.

But good old Harv came through with the best going away present. After the usual jugs of beer he paid for our dinner at the best steak house in town. As I prepared to wend my home he told me he had a surprise for me. He hailed a cab and off we went to Edie's Exotic dancers. I hadn't crossed the threshold of Edie's since Daphne left my life. We found seats along the stage as the lights came up to start the show. The first three girls were passing attractive but looked like they supported enough silicone to start a chip factory. I suggested to Harv we might consider moving on. He said, OK after the next act.

The lights went out and when they came on again a tall blond wearing a white trench coat stood on stage, her back to us. To my wondering amazement the unmistakable Daphne turned to face us. I went goose bumps all over when she winked at me. Her talent and charms stood out as great as ever. She concluded her performance with a double somersault and deposited her last piece of clothing around my neck _ a crimson feather boa. I slept with it that night.

I held Daphne as my last thought as I closed the door to the office and turned in the key. I wanted something good to think about on my last day.

Episode

Dinosaurs Forever?

SCALING NEW HEIGHTS of glory or a lethargic slide into perpetual mediocrity. Whither goest our universities?

I frequent the faculty club less often now I'm no longer a permanent resident of the Crypt. Instead I apply some of the time I once spent over a jug to recreational activities designed to improve my health and extend my time on this worldly orb. I had no word from Harv of late but he is not the sort to make first contact and since I thought I had put in enough time on healthy activity to allow a pint or several the time had come to reconnect.

I found Harv wallowing in a serious grump flattening the cushion of his favorite chair at the faculty club. He peered resolutely into his beer mug as if trying to count the bubbles.

I thought he might put on a display of delight and welcome at my return. Not Harv. It might have been yesterday that we last shared in sudsy conviviality. When I enquired of the woeful countenance he said we teetered on the brink of the abyss and would soon find ourselves hurtling to the bottom, if such existed. I jumped to my feet for a quick look around in case my chair perched on a foundation less secure than I had assumed. A person never knows when the base of a most cherished assumption will disintegrate into clay.

I find an oblique response rather than a frontal assault much safer when Harv is in a doomsday mood. So, I gently asked if he might be more explicit about who, or what, might soon hurtle into the abyss.

"Why the university, as we know it, or to be more accurate, as we thought we knew it."

I waited in silence for more and Harv did not disappoint.

He correctly assumed my ignorance of the origin of the word university and patiently proceeded to fill the gap. He pointed out in slow and careful articulation the Latin origin of the word, '*universitas magistrorum et scholarium.*'

"And the meaning in a language that I and the rest of the world still speak," I asked?

"It means, 'a community of teachers and scholars'. "Don't tell me you never studied Latin," he replied.

Not wanting to disagree I adopted a code of silence on my educational deficit. Without pausing for breath Harv launched into a tale of woe and little hope for our most senior educational institution.

The classrooms are now filled with a set of disengaged students who express their disinterest by neglecting to pick up essays and thereby making any time writing learned and insightful comments in the margins a waste. For them a university education is an entitlement and their degree a birth rite to guarantee a job and middle class life style in perpetuity. The roll of sheepskin, now paper I guess, that is handed over at convocation is the natural outcome of time spent inside the Crypt and not the result of an intellectual journey. The word 'credentialism' describes the entire process. If a little bending of the rules is necessary, once referred to as cheating by the less genteel, so be it, only part of the game. And if done in a collaborative way, even better. It helps build team skills for use in later life. And the hand inside the glove of chicanery is the tide of grade inflation to raise all student boats well above the now discredited gentleman's 'C'. If all that fails students have found that like all citizens they have access to the courts as a last resort. Harv informed me that recently a student at the University of Massachusetts had challenged his 'C' in a federal court. How wonderful I thought, there never cease to exist new and previously undiscovered ways to enrich the legal community.

One apparent reason for the student disengagement and distraction is their focus on developing the real world applicable skill of multi-tasking. It is almost impossible now to find a student who does not fill their day with some money earning activity as well as time over the books. One expert claims the cost to students has increased four times that of inflation in the period, 1990-91 to 2004-05. Get a job has been the response.

Still, the students keep coming to the point that class size and a lack of student faculty contact is a common complaint. Although I don't find it original. I can rarely remember when classes weren't taught in a size that made it impossible to identify more than a few individual students. That is until near the final year of their sentence in the Crypt or further penury in graduate seminars.

But the numbers are necessary to keep the money flowing from the governmental cheque writers and to keep the pipeline flowing has become a full time activity. The heart of the registrar activity is no longer keeping track of students and their grades. No, marketing is where it's at. Rare is the university that has not adopted a marketing program to venture into the high schools across the nation and even abroad to search out and attract the best and brightest. They all go with cheque book in hand and rumour has it that in some cases all a high school grad needs to land a scholarship is a warm body that will show up on day one of classes. Apparently such wooing is now expected and those who do not woo do not win.

The competition is now so intense that is has moved into the lower grades of high school and signings are reported of savvy and talented students in grade 11. If this continues who knows before recruiters are found lurking around kindergarten playgrounds tempting the young with lollipops and cream coloured ponies. Come to think of it, with current advances in genome technology couples may sign up their genes when they get hitched.

In the face of such a list of intractable dilemmas one is left in a quandary of what to do. There is no lack of folk coming up with the first and obvious response. Throw money at the problem and see what sticks. And the more you throw the greater the likelihood some will stick.

Hands are first extended to the government and so it should be since they like to remind us that they are the guardians of educational policy. And they have always been the largest contributor. The claim is still valid but with a much diminished largesse. The nominal dollars may have gone up but the real value of government support has only declined. Many and loud are the calls for redress to former and even larger levels of support.

Not wanting to leave any stone unturned or bank account untapped every Crypt has turned to private donors. An entirely new group of experts occupy some of the prime offices on campus. They are the wealth getters, most often operating under a title that includes the word, 'development'. The head of the group usually obtains the status of a vice-president to ensure requisite prestige and compensation. As far as I can tell they are doing a commendable job of swelling the coffers of the Crypt.

At one time private donors were more than pleased to exchange cash for their name on a scholarship, a building or to stand on the podium at convocation and be handed an honorary degree, thereby allowing the addition of doctor to their business card. The award granted being directly attached to the amount of cash handed over. I understand that now donors are becoming more forthright on how their money may, or may not be spent. A dilemma for the powers that be who think that once the money is in hand the donors not only give up all rights to the cash but also how and to whom it will be doled out.

The research enterprise too has not gone unscathed in these changing times. In what are now bygone days research was what might be termed investigative science. The intellectual pursuit of an idea or problem is what drove the research enterprise. Pecuniary gain did not enter into the equation. Well not beyond the effect on the researcher's advance through the ranks and consequent salary.

Research with a goal of economic gain has crept into the hallowed labs of the Crypt. If there is an advance of intellectual enquiry, so much the better but not of primary concern. The scale and cost of research in science, engineering and medicine has now reached levels where results are demanded. And rewards as great, including I've heard sponsored trips from the drug companies to star researchers who deliver the 'right' results. Under such conditions the question of who owns the research becomes crucial. Matters of intellectual property have emerged from patent offices into the heart of research in the Crypt. And to ensure intellectual property is duly protected offices of legal experts are now part of the research enterprise. They fit in well alongside the marketing experts hired to ensure a full commercial return on research output.

In days now gone by if anyone asked who owned the results of research the answer would be no one, or maybe the world. They would be published and enter the body of universal knowledge for sharing or ignored as happened in most cases. But I do remember one leader of industry mentioning to me over cocktails at a fund raising event that if the academy wished to have their research supported by commercial ventures they may have to become less precious about immediate publishing of potentially commercial results. Maybe that time is upon us.

I remember when the management of a university was placed in the hands of what might be described as a set of reluctant amateurs drawn from the ranks of the faculty. After all, they took academic vows to fulfill a devotion to teaching and research not to that anathema, bureaucracy. Of course the occasional ambitious sole would seek out a position and try to hold onto it in perpetuity but such individuals were looked upon with suspicion, not unlike Cassius of a 'lean and hungry look'. As mentioned earlier in this memoir, a Catch 22 situation where the only person you wanted in an administrative job was someone who didn't want it and the person you definitely didn't want in the job was someone who actively sought it out.

Now such worries are no more as universities take on the image of corporations. The restructured academy has been described as corporatized, privatized, market driven, globalized and commercial. I'm not sure about the outside world but for the most part on the inside world those are not seen as positive words. Where once academics held the senior administrative positions they are increasingly occupied by representatives from the world of commerce to apply their business acumen for greater productivity and cost effectiveness and most importantly, fund raising skills and contacts.

Corporate support services are also being added to the administrative coterie. At the forefront are the marketers to recruit students and assist in the development and sale of research output. And more and more one of the favorite mantras of the marketing professions gains currency, that of branding. If you asked most academics the meaning of branding they would fear the placing of a white hot iron on tender posteriors. But no fear of that since it only applies to setting a university off as distinct from all the rest to attract the necessary _ money, buildings, students and maybe even faculty. But it doesn't end there. At one time it amazed me but no longer when I see ads on TV and bill boards along the roadways proclaiming the wondrous and unique advantages of programs and the universities that house them.

I asked Harv how the faculty was responding to what is no doubt seen as cataclysmic events. Not well was Harv's retort. He claims they are a disillusioned mob, dumped in front of ever larger classes, with minimal contact before an increasingly hostile student body and adjusting badly to demands for gender accommodation. In addition the internet has opened a whole new world of professor ratings beyond the now traditional course evaluations. Harv said there is a new one that rates him and his colleagues on a Hotness scale, including graphics. The rating is according to number of chili peppers from one to five with an extra category at either end. The top end is indicated by a rocket disappearing into space. At the lowest end off the scale to indicate complete cold is a brass monkey minus the obvious. Harv said it should be outlawed. I changed the subject rather than pursue where he might have been placed. To get along the faculty goes along with an endless series of water downed courses that wouldn't challenge a lobotomized cat.

I suggested that maybe the addition of a resilient new group of faculty might help the problem. He suggested I look around the faculty club to evaluate the success in that regard. I noticed an uneven distribution of gray and balding heads filling the chairs. Rather than new faculty the low cost response is contract teachers in positions without any possibility of tenure. I wondered what that meant for a committed faculty united in a common cause of excellence. Of course in my day the only thing you could get the faculty joined in common cause was parking policy.

I suggested that maybe the problem of replacing an aging faculty might be alleviated with the elimination of mandatory retirement.

"Right", Harv grumped. "Lot of good that will do. The only way we'll be able to get rid of the old farts is if their dementia causes them to miss too many classes, or incontinence makes them an embarrassment at the front of the classroom."

On that note I drained the last of the foam from my glass, said thank you but no thank you to Harv's offer to share another jug. I had enough cheer for the afternoon. I'm not sure I'll see Harv again real soon unless I'm feeling too high and need something to bring me back to earth.

I thought what a dismal view for the future of my one time intellectual and working home. It's not that I was ecstatic every moment I was an inmate of the Crypt but when all is said and done it treated me well and it's unlikely I would have found other gainful employment that suited my interests and capability in such fine fashion. It all gave me pause for thought on my return home.

Despite the problems the university faces I have noticed in a variety of public pronouncements that it is seen as the key institution to help us cope with the 21st century. To provide leadership in the rapidly changing world of the information age. To play a role as an engine of economic growth by providing the knowledge that will apply and develop the technology for the changed and competitive world. And I would hope show success in assisting our youth learn the lessons of citizenship and leadership in a renewal of participatory democracy in our society. It will no doubt need financial input from a variety of sources _ public and private but that is not all. One effect of recent changes is an opening of the university at a time where the current inmates have little experience with winds of change blowing from the outside. Their's has been a comfortable life of internal change, if any.

Upon reflection I'm more optimistic about the future of all dear old Crypts. After all it is one of the world's three oldest continuing institutions over the centuries. The others are the church and the third is one habited mainly by the female sex. I think they too will go on and adjust but I will comment on neither here. However, the university emerged from its ecclesiastical beginnings to adopt a research role in the 18th century and further adapted to the Humboldt revolution that consolidated the role of research in the 19th century. I'm sure such resiliency is still possible. It is my experience that one should never underestimate the entrepreneurial skills of the inhabitants of a Crypt.

It reminds me of what Oscar Wilde once said in a different context:

"The truth is rarely pure and never simple. Modern life would be very tedious if it were either."

Life within the Crypt should never be simple, nor tedious.

I would now like to end with words from the great thespian and philosopher William Claude Dunkenfield, a.k.a. W. C. Fields. Not hard to see why he went for the abbreviated version. How else could he get his name on a marquee?

"The reports of my demise have been greatly exaggerated."

So shall it be for the university.